The Living Stream

The Living Stream

An Anthology
of Twentieth Century Verse

compiled by

JANET ADAM SMITH

FABER AND FABER
London

First published in 1969
by Faber and Faber Limited
24 Russell Square London WC1
Printed in Great Britain by
Latimer Trend & Co Ltd Plymouth

SBN (hard bound edition) 571 09062 1
SBN (paper bound edition) 571 09064 8

NOTE ON ARRANGEMENT

INTRODUCTION   *page* 7

THE POEMS   11
    In alphabetical order of first lines

CONNECTIONS   164
    Some suggested groupings of poems; every poem
    mentioned has its page number

AUTHOR INDEX   174
    Poets by alphabetical order, with the
    titles of the books the poems come from, and a
    few biographical or other facts that are
    relevant to an understanding of the context
    or occasion of a poem

TITLE INDEX   189
    The first page reference will be to the
    text of the poem, the rest to any
    mentions of it in Connections or in
    the notes in the Author Index

ACKNOWLEDGEMENT

Many people—teachers, pupils, poets, readers—have helped me with the making of this anthology. I thank them all, particularly two with whom I have discussed the project at various stages, whose comments and criticisms have helped me to clear my own mind: Mr. John Field (who also suggested the title of the collection) and Mr. Harold Rosen.

J.A.S.

INTRODUCTION

I want first to declare what this collection of poems is not. It is not a map of modern poetry, with Mount Eliot and the Yeats Range given their due heights and the lesser hills shaded in. I have not tried to represent each poet "fairly" according to some ideal Ranking List; many good poets of the last forty years are not here at all. Nor have I tried to make the collection a historical survey, showing how modern poetry has developed and who has "influenced" whom.

What I have tried to do is to give the reader some notion of the scope and modes of modern poetry, in subject, attitude, language, rhythm, tone and imagery; to present a range of voices. I want to introduce readers to poems rather than to poets.

With these aims in view, the best arrangement seemed to be a simple alphabetical order by first lines, with the author's name at the foot of each poem. In this way attention is focused on the poem itself as a whole, rather than on the poet (as it tends to be when poems are grouped by authors) or on subject (as when poems are grouped by theme). I look on this alphabetical presentation as the equivalent, in a book, of the teacher handing out separate cyclostyled poems to the class. A poem thus presented challenges the reader, makes him ask questions: What *is* this poem? Who is speaking? How do I say it? What does it say? The poem should be a unique experience, demanding a fresh response—not another poem by Yeats, not another poem about cats, to be met with the same response as the poem on the page before.

To categorize a poem by its manifest subject is to box it up in only one of its possible characters. To put in a pen labelled "Animal

7

Poems", Ted Hughes's "A Dream of Horses" (which is also about power and glory), Vachel Lindsay's "The Flower-fed Buffaloes" (which is also about the conquest of a continent) and Richard Eberhart's "Hoot Owls" (which is also about our idea of the poetical) is as limiting as the newspapers' way of labelling as Housewife a person who may also be a painter and a tennis player.

It is the permanence of grouping by subject within a book that I distrust. There the poems are, bedded down in the same category, uneasy bedfellows perhaps but unable to part till the edition of the book runs out. But to present the poems in a way that stresses their separateness, their uniqueness, does not of course mean that there is no value in making connections between one poem and another. A look at two poems together will often give a starting-point for discussion; and often, by emphasizing differences within a general likeness, sharpen a reader's sense of the individuality of each. Only, such connections should be fluid, and not exclusive. Connect Louis MacNeice's "Bagpipe Music" with John Manifold's "Fife Tune" because in both the poet is finding in words an equivalent for the sound of an instrument; but connect also "Bagpipe Music" with the same poet's "Birmingham" because both poems build up, under the aural or visual surface, a sense of the preoccupations and values of a particular community. George Mackay Brown's "The Funeral of Ally Flett" connects with John Crowe Ransom's "Dead Boy", for in both poems a death is seen in the context of a close-knit society; but "Ally Flett" also connects with Dylan Thomas's "Fern Hill" in being a celebration of life. At the end of the book I have suggested some of the connections that struck me; I hope that many more will be made by teachers and pupils as part of their personal exploration of the poems.

I should like to think of both teachers and class as setting out together on each poem as on a journey of exploration—the teacher being not the person with all the answers to the "problems" and "difficulties" of the poem, but the reader with the greatest experience. They will have some standard equipment to help them, such as dictionaries of words and myths; but their most important equipment will be their own eyes and ears, imagination and experience. They will be exploring the meanings and possibilities of words; following the development of images; testing beat and rhythm and finding new patterns of sound—a reading aloud should

8

be part of the exploration; recognizing known experiences, feelings and attitudes, and discovering new ones.

Each poem is here, in its own right, chosen primarily because I liked it and thought it good in its own mode, and not because it "represented" a movement or "illustrated" a theme. I do not expect you, the reader, to like every one; it would be surprising if you were to share my likings exactly. But if a poem repels you, do not just pass on. Look at it again and ask yourself: Is it because it's a subject that you don't much want to think about, like the death of a parent? Is it because you don't like what the poet seems to be expressing—or is he really speaking through some character, like Betjeman's lady in "Westminster Abbey", and making a portrait of her by representing her views and prejudices? Is it because a poem upsets your notions of what's fitting; does Iain Crichton Smith's "Old Woman" jolt you because you think that old age (in poetry anyway) should be "serene and bright, And lovely as a Lapland night"? Is it because the poem seems to be forcing you to reappraise your attitudes—say about war, work or love—or your ideas of what poetry should be?

Poetry can call for a disturbance of our attitudes that can be painful; but a poem that begins by disturbing may end by delighting. It can be like the knockers on the door in D. H. Lawrence's "Song of a Man Who Has Come Through":

> *What is the knocking?*
> *What is the knocking at the door in the night?*
> *It is somebody wants to do us harm.*
>
> *No, no, it is the three strange angels.*
> *Admit them, admit them.*

JANET ADAM SMITH

9

The Pay is Good

A class of thirty student engineers,
Sixteen years old, disliked by all the staff.
Hearing about them at the interview,
And told to rule them with a rod of iron,
I tried my best but found I could not laugh.

He might be wrong. But I, no raw recruit,
Had found a proverb in a classroom war:
The peaceful sheriff proves that he can shoot
Before he throws his gunbelt on the floor.

A month or so of brooding self-distrust,
And then the moment came. I reached the door
(So this is it. Fight, for the love of Kell.
Show them who's boss—there's no going back—you must)—
And flung it open on the core of hell.

Somehow it worked. And they will never know
By what dissimulation it was done;
Or how the fuse of terror blasted out
Courage enough to master thirty-one.

RICHARD KELL

Miss Robinson's Funeral

A cold afternoon, and death looks prouder
As mourning motors mourning motors follow,
One solemn as another. Lilies shiver,
Carnations also shiver, while the hollow
Seagulls search for offal in the river
And a woman burrows in her bag for powder.

The undertakers don't observe the scenery
And nothing moves them but the wheels they glide on,
The undertakers undertake to bury
(How black the motor cars they ride on),
They are not volatile or sad or merry,
Neither are waxworks going by machinery.

The coffin's full, and the time is after four;
The grave is empty, earth joins earth once more—
But the ghost of the late Miss Robinson is floating
Backside upwards in the air with a smile across her jaw:
She was tickled to death, and is carefully noting
Phenomena she never thought of noticing before.

WILLIAM PLOMER

Old Man Playing with Children

A discreet householder exclaims on the grandsire
In warpaint and feathers, with fierce grandsons and axes
Dancing round a backyard fire of boxes:
"Watch grandfather, he'll set the house on fire."

But I will unriddle for you the thought of his mind,
An old one you cannot open with conversation.
What animates the thin legs in risky motion?
Mixes the snow on the head with snow on the wind?

"Grandson, grandsire. We are equally boy and boy.
Do not offer your reclining-chair and slippers
With tedious old women talking in wrappers.
This life is not good but in danger and in joy.

"It is you the elder to these and younger to me
Who are penned as slaves by properties and causes
And never walk from your insupportable houses
And shamefully, when boys shout, go in and flee.

"May God forgive me, I know your middling ways,
Having taken care and performed ignominies unreckoned
Between the first brief childhood and the brief second,
But I will be more honorable in these days."

JOHN CROWE RANSOM

Of Cats

A heart constituted wholly of cats
(Even as the family nose derives)
From father and mother a child inherits,
And every cat gets fully nine lives.

Wildest cats, with scruff cats, queenly cats
(Crowned), they jig to violins; they go stately
Where a torched pageantry celebrates
A burial, or crowning (of a cat); or sing sweetly

At your ears and in harmony left with right
Till the moon bemoods: to the new, to the full,
Only look up: possessing night—
Cattic Bacchanal! A world of wild lamps and wauling,

A world gone to the cats, every cat of the heart out,
And darkness and light a cat upon a cat—
They have outwitted our nimblest wits.
One who, one night, sank a cat in a sack

With a stone to the canal-bottom
(Under the bridge, in the very belly of the black)
And hurried a mile home
Found that cat on the doorstep waiting for him.

So are we all held in utter mock by the cats.

TED HUGHES

Tramp

A knock at the door
And he stands there,
A tramp with his can
Asking for tea,
Strong for a poor man
On his way—where?

He looks at his feet,
I look at the sky;
Over us the planes build
The shifting rafters
Of that new world
We have sworn by.

I sleep in my bed,
He sleeps in the old
Dead leaves of a ditch.
My dreams are haunted;
Are his dreams rich?
If I wake early,
He wakes cold.

R. S. THOMAS

Musée des Beaux Arts

About suffering they were never wrong,
The Old Masters: how well they understood
Its human position; how it takes place
While someone else is eating or opening a window or just
    walking dully along;
How, when the aged are reverently, passionately waiting
For the miraculous birth, there always must be
Children who did not specially want it to happen, skating
On a pond at the edge of the wood:
They never forgot
That even the dreadful martyrdom must run its course
Anyhow in a corner, some untidy spot
Where the dogs go on with their doggy life and the torturer's
    horse
Scratches its innocent behind on a tree.

In Breughel's *Icarus*, for instance: how everything turns
    away
Quite leisurely from the disaster; the ploughman may
Have heard the splash, the forsaken cry,
But for him it was not an important failure; the sun shone
As it had to on the white legs disappearing into the green
Water; and the expensive delicate ship that must have seen
Something amazing, a boy falling out of the sky,
Had somewhere to get to and sailed calmly on.

W. H. AUDEN

The Express

After the first powerful, plain manifesto
The black statement of pistons, without more fuss
But gliding like a queen, she leaves the station.
Without bowing and with restrained unconcern
She passes the houses which humbly crowd outside,
The gasworks, and at last the heavy page
Of death, printed by gravestones in the cemetery.
Beyond the town, there lies the open country
Where, gathering speed, she acquires mystery,
The luminous self-possession of ships on ocean.
It is now she begins to sing—at first quite low
Then loud, and at last with a jazzy madness—
The song of her whistle screaming at curves,
Of deafening tunnels, brakes, innumerable bolts.
And always light, aerial, underneath,
Retreats the elate metre of her wheels.
Steaming through metal landscape on her lines
She plunges new eras of white happiness
Where speed throws up strange shapes, broad curves
And parallels clean like trajectories from guns.
At last, further than Edinburgh or Rome,
Beyond the crest of the world, she reaches night
Where only a low stream-line brightness
Of phosphorus on the tossing hills is light.
Ah, like a comet through flame, she moves entranced
Wrapt in her music no bird song, no, nor bough
Breaking with honey buds, shall ever equal.

STEPHEN SPENDER

Cynddylan on a Tractor

Ah, you should see Cynddylan on a tractor.
Gone the old look that yoked him to the soil;
He's a new man now, part of the machine,
His nerves of metal and his blood oil.
The clutch curses, but the gears obey
His least bidding, and lo, he's away
Out of the farmyard, scattering hens.
Riding to work now as a great man should,
He is the knight at arms breaking the fields'
Mirror of silence, emptying the wood
Of foxes and squirrels and bright jays.
The sun comes over the tall trees
Kindling all the hedges, but not for him
Who runs his engine on a different fuel.
And all the birds are singing, bills wide in vain,
As Cynddylan passes proudly up the lane.

R. S. THOMAS

Giorno dei Morti

Along the avenue of cypresses,
All in their scarlet cloaks and surplices
Of linen, go the chanting choristers,
The priests in gold and black, the villagers . . .

And all along the path to the cemetery
The round dark heads of men crowd silently,
And black-scarved faces of womenfolk, wistfully
Watch at the banner of death, and the mystery.

And at the foot of a grave a father stands
With sunken head; and forgotten, folded hands;
And at the foot of a grave a mother kneels
With pale shut face, nor either hears nor feels

The coming of the chanting choristers
Between the avenue of cypresses,
The silence of the many villagers,
The candle-flames beside the surplices.

D. H. LAWRENCE

Waterfalls

Always in that valley in Wales I hear the noise
  Of waters falling.
                There is a clump of trees
    We climbed for nuts; and high in the trees the boys
      Lost in the rookery's cries
          Would cross, and branches cracking under their
             knees

Would break, and make in the winter wood new gaps.
  The leafmould covering the ground was almost black,
    But speckled and striped were the nuts we threw in our caps,
      Milked from split shells and cups,
          Secret as chestnuts when they are tipped from a sack,

Glossy and new.
             Always in that valley in Wales
I hear that sound, those voices. They keep fresh
  What ripens, falls, drops into darkness, fails,
    Gone when dawn shines on scales,
      And glides from village memory, slips through the
        mesh,

And is not, when we come again.
                I look:
  Voices are under the bridge, and that voice calls,
    Now late, and answers;
              then, as the light twigs break
    Back, there is only the brook
      Reminding the stones where, under a breath, it falls.

VERNON WATKINS

Next, Please

Always too eager for the future, we
Pick up bad habits of expectancy.
Something is always approaching; every day
Till then we say,

Watching from a bluff the tiny, clear,
Sparkling armada of promises draw near.
How slow they are! And how much time they waste,
Refusing to make haste!

Yet still they leave us holding wretched stalks
Of disappointment, for, though nothing balks
Each big approach, leaning with brasswork prinked,
Each rope distinct,

Flagged, and the figurehead with golden tits
Arching our way, it never anchors; it's
No sooner present than it turns to past.
Right to the last

We think each one will heave to and unload
All good into our lives, all we are owed
For waiting so devoutly and so long.
But we are wrong:

Only one ship is seeking us, a black-
Sailed unfamiliar, towing at her back
A huge and birdless silence. In her wake
No waters breed or break.

PHILIP LARKIN

Old Woman

And she, being old, fed from a mashed plate
as an old mare might droop across a fence
to the dull pastures of its ignorance.
Her husband held her upright while he prayed

to God who is all-forgiving to send down
some angel somewhere who might land perhaps
in his foreign wings among the gradual crops.
She munched, half dead, blindly searching the spoon.

Outside, the grass was raging. There I sat
imprisoned in my pity and my shame
that men and women having suffered time
should sit in such a place, in such a state

and wished to be away, yes, to be far away
with athletes, heroes, Greeks or Roman men
who pushed their bitter spears into a vein
and would not spend an hour with such decay.

"Pray God", he said, "we ask you, God", he said.
The bowed back was quiet. I saw the teeth
tighten their grip around a delicate death.
And nothing moved within the knotted head

but only a few poor veins as one might see
vague wishless seaweed floating on a tide
of all the salty waters where had died
too many waves to mark two more or three.

IAIN CRICHTON-SMITH

A Ballad for Katharine of Aragon

Queen of England, 1509–1533
Buried in Peterborough Cathedral

As I walked down by the river
Down by the frozen fen
I saw the grey cathedral
With the eyes of a child of ten.
O the railway arch is smoky
As the Flying Scot goes by
And but for the Education Act
Go Jumper Cross and I.

But war is a bitter bugle
That all must learn to blow
And it didn't take long to stop the song
In the dirty Italian snow.
O war is a casual mistress
And the world is her double bed
She has a few charms in her mechanised arms
But you wake up and find yourself dead.

The olive tree in winter
Casts her banner down
And the priest in white and scarlet
Comes up from the muddy town.
O never more will Jumper
Watch the Flying Scot go by
His funeral knell was a six-inch shell
Singing across the sky.

The Queen of Castile has a daughter
Who won't come home again
She lies in the grey cathedral
Under the arms of Spain.
O the Queen of Castile has a daughter
Torn out by the roots
Her lovely breast in a cold stone chest
Under the farmers' boots.

Now I like a Spanish party
And many O many the day
I have watched them swim as the night came dim
In Algeciras Bay,
O the high sierra was thunder
And the seven-branched river of Spain
Came down to the sea to plunder
The heart of the sailor again.

O shall I leap in the river
And knock upon paradise door
For a gunner of twenty-seven and a half
And a queen of twenty-four?
From the almond tree by the river
I watch the sky with a groan
For Jumper and Kate are always out late
And I lie here alone.

CHARLES CAUSLEY

Mother and Son

At nine o'clock in the morning
My son said to me:
Mother, he said, from the wet streets
The clouds are removed and the sun walks
Without shoes on the warm pavements.
There are girls biddable at the corners
With teeth cleaner than your white plates;
The sharp clatter of your dishes
Is less pleasant to me than their laughter.
The day is building; before its bright walls
Fall in dust, let me go
Beyond the front garden without you
To find glasses unstained by tears,
To find mirrors that do not reproach
My smooth face; to hear above the town's
Din life roaring in the veins.

R. S. THOMAS

The Scholars

Bald heads forgetful of their sins,
Old, learned, respectable bald heads
Edit and annotate the lines
That young men, tossing on their beds,
Rhymed out in love's despair
To flatter beauty's ignorant ear.

All shuffle there; all cough in ink;
All wear the carpet with their shoes;
All think what other people think;
All know the man their neighbour knows.
Lord, what would they say
Did their Catullus walk that way?

W. B. YEATS

The Funeral of Ally Flett

Because of his long pilgrimage
  From pub to alehouse
    And all the liquor laws he'd flout,
Being under age
  And wringing peatbog spirits from a clout
Into a secret kettle,
  And making every Sabbath a carouse,
Mansie brought a twelve-year bottle.

Because his shy foot turned aside
  From Merran's door,
    And Olga's coat with the red button
And Inga's side
  Naked as snow or swan or wild bog cotton
Made him laugh loud
  And after, spit with scunner on the floor,
Marget sewed a long chaste shroud.

Because the scythe was in the oats
  When he lay flat,
    And Jean Macdonald's best March ale
Cooled the long throats
  (At noon the reapers drank from the common pail)
And Sanders said
  "Corn enough here for every tramp and rat,"
Sigrid baked her lightest bread.

Although the fleet from Hamnavoe
  Drew heavy nets
    Off Noup Head, in a squall of rain,
Turning in slow
  Gull-haunted circles near the three-mile line,
And mouthing cod
  Went iced and salted into slippery crates,
One skipper heard and bowed his head.

Because at Dounby and the fair
   Twelve tearaways
      Brought every copper in the islands
Round their uproar
   And this one made a sweet and sudden silence
Like that white bird
   That broke the tempest with a twig of praise,
The preacher spoke the holy word.

Because the hour of grass is brief
   And the red rose
      Is a bare thorn in the east wind
And a strong life
   Runs out and spends itself like barren sand
And the dove dies
   And every loveliest lilt must have a close,
Old Betsy came with bitter cries.

Because his dance was gathered now
   And parish feet
      Went blundering their separate roads
After the plough
   And after net and peat and harvest loads,
Yet from the cradle
   Their fated steps with a fixed passion beat,
Tammas brought his Swedish fiddle.

GEORGE MACKAY BROWN

Lullaby

Beloved, may your sleep be sound
That have found it where you fed.
What were all the world's alarms
To mighty Paris when he found
Sleep upon a golden bed
That first dawn in Helen's arms?

Sleep, beloved, such a sleep
As did that wild Tristram know
When, the potion's work being done,
Roe could run or doe could leap
Under oak and beechen bough,
Roe could leap or doe could run.

Such a sleep and sound as fell
Upon Eurotas' grassy bank
When the holy bird, that there
Accomplished his predestined will,
From the limbs of Leda sank
But not from her protecting care.

W. B. YEATS

Better One Golden Lyric

Better a'e gowden lyric
Than a social problem solved
Tho' maist folk never see
The beauty that's evolved
And think a million times mair
nauseating — O' their ain waugh welfare.

Better a'e gowden lyric
That nane but the poets see
Than a Messiah's praise in a day
The mob in its vain moods gies
In turn to a Prince or jockey,
A Tancy, or Jennie Lee.

Better a'e gowden lyric
The mob'll never ken
For this in the last resort
Mak's them less apes, mair men,
And leads their leaders albeit
They're owre blin' to see it.

Better a'e gowden lyric
Than Insurance, Bankin', and Law,
Better a'e gowden lyric
Than the Castle's soarin' wa';
Better a'e gowden lyric
at all — Than onything else ava!

HUGH MacDIARMID

Digging

Between my finger and my thumb
The squat pen rests; snug as a gun.

Under my window, a clean rasping sound
When the spade sinks into gravelly ground:
My father, digging. I look down

Till his straining rump among the flowerbeds
Bends low, comes up twenty years away
Stooping in rhythm through potato drills
Where he was digging.

The coarse boot nestled on the lug, the shaft
Against the inside knee was levered firmly.
He rooted out tall tops, buried the bright edge deep
To scatter new potatoes that we picked
Loving their cool hardness in our hands.

By God, the old man could handle a spade.
Just like his old man.

My grandfather cut more turf in a day
Than any other man on Toner's bog.
Once I carried him milk in a bottle
Corked sloppily with paper. He straightened up
To drink it, then fell right away
Nicking and slicing neatly, heaving sods
Over his shoulder, going down and down
For the good turf. Digging.

The cold smell of potato mould, the squelch and slap
Of soggy peat, the curt cuts of an edge

Through living roots awaken in my head.
But I've no spade to follow men like them.

Between my finger and my thumb
The squat pen rests.
I'll dig with it.

SEAMUS HEANEY

Perseus

Borrowed wings on his ankles,
Carrying a stone death,
The hero entered the hall,
All in the hall looked up,
Their breath frozen on them,
And there was no more shuffle or clatter in the hall at all.

So a friend of a man comes in
And leaves a book he is lending or flowers
And goes again, alive but as good as dead,
And you are left alive, no better than dead,
And you dare not turn the leaden pages of the book or touch
    the flowers, the hooded and arrested hours.

Close your eyes,
There are suns beneath your lids,
Or look in the looking-glass in the end room—
You will find it full of eyes,
The ancient smiles of men cut out with scissors and kept in
    mirrors.

Ever to meet me comes, in sun or dull,
The gay hero swinging the Gorgon's head
And I am left, with the dull drumming of the sun,
    suspended and dead,
Or the dumb grey-brown of the day is a leper's cloth,
And one feels the earth going round and round the globe
    of the blackening mantle, a mad moth.

LOUIS MACNEICE

The Bridge of Dread

But when you reach the Bridge of Dread
Your flesh will huddle into its nest
For refuge and your naked head
Creep in the casement of your breast,

And your great bulk grow thin and small
And cower within its cage of bone,
While dazed you watch your footsteps crawl
Toadlike across the leagues of stone.

If they come, you will not feel
About your feet the adders slide,
For still your head's demented wheel
Whirls on your neck from side to side

Searching for danger. Nothing there.
And yet your breath will whistle and beat
As on you push the stagnant air
That breaks in rings about your feet

Like dirty suds. If there should come
Some bodily terror to that place,
Great knotted serpents dread and dumb,
You would accept it as a grace.

Until you see a burning wire
Shoot from the ground. As in a dream
You'll wonder at that flower of fire,
That weed caught in a burning beam.

And you are past. Remember then,
Fix deep within your dreaming head
Year, hour or endless moment when
You reached and crossed the Bridge of Dread.

EDWIN MUIR

A Polished Performance

Citizens of the polished capital
   Sigh for the towns up country,
And their innocent simplicity.

People in the towns up country
   Applaud the unpolished innocence
Of the distant villages.

Dwellers in the distant villages
   Speak of a simple unspoilt girl,
Living alone, deep in the bush.

Deep in the bush we found her,
   Large and innocent of eye,
Among gentle gibbons and mountain ferns.

Perfect for the part, perfect,
   Except for the dropsy
Which comes from polished rice.

In the capital our film is much admired,
   Its gentle gibbons and mountain ferns,
Unspoilt, unpolished, large and innocent of eye.

D. J. ENRIGHT

Her Husband

Comes home dull with coal-dust deliberately
To grime the sink and foul towels and let her
Learn with scrubbing brush and scrubbing board
The stubborn character of money.

And let her learn through what kind of dust
He has earned his thirst and the right to quench it
And what sweat he has exchanged for his money
And the blood-weight of money. He'll humble her

With new light on her obligations.
The fried, woody chips, kept warm two hours in the oven,
Are only part of her answer.
Hearing the rest, he slams them to the fire back

And is away round the house-end singing
"Come back to Sorrento" in a voice
Of resounding corrugated iron.
Her back has bunched into a hump as an insult.

For they will have their rights.
Their jurors are to be assembled
From the little crumbs of soot. Their brief
Goes straight up to heaven and nothing more is heard of it.

TED HUGHES

36

The Face in the Mirror

Grey haunted eyes, absent-mindedly glaring
From wide, uneven orbits; one brow drooping
Somewhat over the eye
Because of a missile fragment still inhering,
Skin deep, as a foolish record of old-world fighting.

Crookedly broken nose—low tackling caused it;
Cheeks, furrowed; coarse grey hair, flying frenetic;
Forehead, wrinkled and high;
Jowls, prominent; ears, large; jaw, pugilistic;
Teeth, few; lips, full and ruddy; mouth, ascetic.

I pause with razor poised, scowling derision
At the mirrored man whose beard needs my attention,
And once more ask him why
He still stands ready, with a boy's presumption,
To court the queen in her high silk pavilion.

ROBERT GRAVES

The Goodnight

He stood still by her bed
Watching his daughter breathe,
The dark and silver head,
The fingers curled beneath,
And thought: Though she may have
Intelligence and charm
And luck, they will not save
Her life from every harm.

The lives of children are
Dangerous to their parents
With fire, water, air,
And other accidents;
And some, for a child's sake,
Anticipating doom,
Empty the world to make
The world safe as a room.

Who could endure the pain
That was Laocoön's?
Twisting, he saw again
In the same coil his sons.
Plumed in his father's skill,
Young Icarus flew higher
Toward the sun, until
He fell in rings of fire.

A man who cannot stand
Children's perilous play,
With lifted voice and hand
Drives the children away.
Out of sight, out of reach,
The tumbling children pass;
He sits on an empty beach,
Holding an empty glass.

Who said that tenderness
Will turn the heart to stone?
May I endure her weakness
As I endure my own.
Better to say goodnight
To breathing flesh and blood
Each night as though the night
Were always only good.

LOUIS SIMPSON

Twice Shy

Her scarf *à la* Bardot,
In suede flats for the walk,
She came with me one evening
For air and friendly talk.
We crossed the quiet river,
Took the embankment walk.

Traffic holding its breath,
Sky a tense diaphragm:
Dusk hung like a backcloth
That shook where a swan swam,
Tremulous as a hawk
Hanging deadly, calm.

A vacuum of need
Collapsed each hunting heart
But tremulously we held
As hawk and prey apart,
Preserved classic decorum,
Deployed our talk with art.

Our juvenilia
Had taught us both to wait,
Not to publish feeling
And regret it all too late—
Mushroom loves already
Had puffed and burst in hate.

So, chary and excited
As a thrush linked on a hawk,
We thrilled to the March twilight
With nervous childish talk:
Still waters running deep
Along the embankment walk.

SEAMUS HEANEY

Rannoch, by Glencoe

Here the crow starves, here the patient stag
Breeds for the rifle. Between the soft moor
And the soft sky, scarcely room
To leap or soar. Substance crumbles, in the thin air
Moon cold or moon hot. The road winds in
Listlessness of ancient war,
Languor of broken steel,
Clamour of confused wrong, apt
In silence. Memory is strong
Beyond the bone. Pride snapped,
Shadow of pride is long, in the long pass
No concurrence of bone.

T. S. ELIOT

What Then?

His chosen comrades thought at school
He must grow a famous man;
He thought the same and lived by rule,
All his twenties crammed with toil;
"What then?" sang Plato's ghost. "What then?"

Everything he wrote was read,
After certain years he won
Sufficient money for his need,
Friends that have been friends indeed;
"What then?" sang Plato's ghost. "What then?"

All his happier dreams came true—
A small old house, wife, daughter, son,
Grounds where plum and cabbage grew,
Poets and Wits about him drew;
"What then?" sang Plato's ghost. "What then?"

"The work is done", grown old he thought,
"According to my boyish plan;
Let the fools rage, I swerved in naught,
Something to perfection brought";
But louder sang that ghost, "What then?"

W. B. YEATS

Lost Love

His eyes are quickened so with grief,
He can watch a grass or leaf
Every instant grow; he can
Clearly through a flint wall see,
Or watch the startled spirit flee
From the throat of a dead man.
   Across two counties he can hear
And catch your words before you speak.
The woodlouse or the maggot's weak
Clamour rings in his sad ear,
And noise so slight it would surpass
Credence—drinking sound of grass,
Worm talk, clashing jaws of moth
Chumbling holes in cloth;
The groan of ants who undertake
Gigantic loads for honour's sake
(Their sinews creak, their breath comes thin):
Whir of spiders when they spin,
And minute whispering, mumbling, sighs
Of idle grubs and flies.
   This man is quickened so with grief,
He wanders god-like or like thief
Inside and out, below, above,
Without relief seeking lost love.

ROBERT GRAVES

Edinburgh Courtyard in July

Hot light is smeared as thick as paint
On these ramshackle tenements. Stones smell
　Of dust. Their hoisting into quaint
Crowsteps, corbels, carved with fool and saint,
Holds fathoms of heat, like water in a well.

Cliff-dwellers have poked out from their
High cave-mouths brilliant rags on drying-lines;
　They hang still, dazzling in the glare,
And lead the eye up, ledge by ledge, to where
A chimney's tilted helmet winks and shines.

And water from a broken drain
Splashes a glassy hand out in the air
　That breaks in an unbraiding rain
And falls still fraying, to become a stain
That spreads by footsteps, ghosting everywhere.

NORMAN MacCAIG

Question and Answer

"How do you love me, with silver and gold?"
"How do you love me, with kisses untold?"
"How do you love me?", again and again.

"I love you with passion and fury and pain,
With death at my elbow, and none to explain
The pain and the passion, where out in the rain
A lover lies dreaming of silver and gold,
And cold heavy raindrops are kisses untold."

MICHAEL ROBERTS

Piazza di Spagna, Early Morning

I can't forget
How she stood at the top of that long marble stair
Amazed, and then with a sleepy pirouette
Went dancing slowly down to the fountain-quieted square;

Nothing upon her face
But some impersonal loveliness,—not then a girl,
But as it were a reverie of the place,
A called-for falling glide and whirl;

As when a leaf, petal, or thin chip
Is drawn to the falls of a pool and, circling a moment above it,
Rides on over the lip—
Perfectly beautiful, perfectly ignorant of it.

RICHARD WILBUR

45

The Heroes

I dreamed of war-heroes, of wounded war-heroes
With just enough of their charms shot away
To make them more handsome. The women moved nearer
To touch their brave wounds and their hair streaked with grey.

I saw them in long ranks ascending the gang-planks;
The girls with the doughnuts were cheerful and gay.
They minded their manners and muttered their thanks;
The Chaplain advised them to watch and to pray.

They shipped these rapscallions, these sea-sick battalions
To a patriotic and picturesque spot;
They gave them new bibles and marksmen's medallions,
Compasses, maps, and committed the lot.

A fine dust has settled on all that scrap metal.
The heroes were packaged and sent home in parts
To pluck at a poppy and sew on a petal
And count the long night by the stroke of their hearts.

LOUIS SIMPSON

Easter Poem

I had gone on Easter Day
early and alone to be
beyond insidious bells
(that any other Sunday
I'd not hear) up to the hills
where are winds to blow away

commination. In the frail
first light I saw him, unreal
and sudden through lifting mist,
a fox on a barn door, nailed
like a coloured plaster Christ
in a Spanish shrine, his tail

coiled around his loins. Sideways
his head hung limply, his ears
snagged with burdock, his dry nose
plugged with black blood. For two days
he'd held the orthodox pose.
The endemic English noise

of Easter Sunday morning
was mixed in the mist swirling
and might have moved his stiff head.
Under the hill the ringing
had begun: and the sun rose red
on the stains of his bleeding.

I walked the length of the day's
obsession. At dusk I was
swallowed by the misted barn,
sucked by the peristalsis
of my fear that he had gone,
leaving nails for souvenirs.

But he was there still. I saw
no sign. He hung as before.
Only the wind had risen
to comb the thorns from his fur.
I left my superstition
stretched on the banging barn door.

TED WALKER

Easter 1916

I have met them at close of day
Coming with vivid faces
From counter or desk among grey
Eighteenth-century houses.
I have passed with a nod of the head
Or polite meaningless words,
Or have lingered awhile and said
Polite meaningless words,
And I thought before I had done
Of a mocking tale or a gibe
To please a companion
Around the fire at the club,
Being certain that they and I
But lived where motley is worn:
All changed, changed utterly:
A terrible beauty is born.

That woman's days were spent
In ignorant good-will,
Her nights in argument
Until her voice grew shrill.
What voice more sweet than hers

48

When, young and beautiful,
She rode to harriers?
This man had kept a school
And rode our wingèd horse;
This other his helper and friend
Was coming into his force;
He might have won fame in the end,
So sensitive his nature seemed,
So daring and sweet his thought.
This other man I had dreamed
A drunken, vainglorious lout.
He had done most bitter wrong
To some who are near my heart,
Yet I number him in the song;
He, too, has resigned his part
In the casual comedy;
He, too, has been changed in his turn,
Transformed utterly:
A terrible beauty is born.

Hearts with one purpose alone
Through summer and winter seem
Enchanted to a stone
To trouble the living stream.
The horse that comes from the road,
The rider, the birds that range
From cloud to tumbling cloud,
Minute by minute they change;
A shadow of cloud on the stream
Changes minute by minute;
A horse-hoof slides on the brim,
And a horse plashes within it;
The long-legged moor-hens dive,
And hens to moor-cocks call;
Minute by minute they live:
The stone's in the midst of all.

Too long a sacrifice
Can make a stone of the heart.
O when may it suffice?
That is Heaven's part, our part
To murmur name upon name,
As a mother names her child
When sleep at last has come
On limbs that had run wild.
What is it but nightfall?
No, no, not night but death;
Was it needless death after all?
For England may keep faith
For all that is done and said.
We know their dream; enough
To know they dreamed and are dead;
And what if excess of love
Bewildered them till they died?
I write it out in a verse—
MacDonagh and MacBride
And Connolly and Pearse
Now and in time to be,
Wherever green is worn,
Are changed, changed utterly:
A terrible beauty is born.

September 25 1916

W. B. YEATS

Mid-Term Break

I sat all morning in the college sick bay
Counting bells knelling classes to a close.
At two o'clock our neighbours drove me home.

In the porch I met my father crying—
He had always taken funerals in his stride—
And Big Jim Evans saying it was a hard blow.

The baby cooed and laughed and rocked the pram
When I came in, and I was embarrassed
By old men standing up to shake my hand

And tell me they were "sorry for my trouble",
Whispers informed strangers I was the eldest,
Away at school, as my mother held my hand

In hers and coughed out angry tearless sighs.
At ten o'clock the ambulance arrived
With the corpse, stanched and bandaged by the nurses.

Next morning I went up into the room. Snowdrops
And candles soothed the bedside; I saw him
For the first time in six weeks. Paler now,

Wearing a poppy bruise on his left temple,
He lay in the four foot box as in his cot.
No gaudy scars, the bumper knocked him clear.

A four foot box, a foot for every year.

SEAMUS HEANEY

Me and the Animals

I share my kneebones with the gnat,
My joints with ferrets, eyes with rat
Or blind bat, blinking owl, the goat
His golden cloven orb. I mate like a stoat,
Or like the heavy whale, that moves a sea
To make a mother's gross fecundity.

I share lung's action with the snake;
The fish is cold, but vertebrate like me; my steak
Is muscle from a butcher's arm, a butcher's heart
Is some sheep's breast that throbbed; I start
At noise with ears which in a dog
Can hear what I cannot; in water I'm a frog.

I differ most in lacking their content
To be, no more. They're at mercy of the scent,
Of hot, cold, summer, winter, hunger, anger,
Or ritual establishing the herd, smelling out the stranger:
I walk upright, alone, ungoverned, free;
Yet their occasional lust, fear, unease, walk with me
Always. All ways.

DAVID HOLBROOK

For No Good Reason

I walk on the waste-ground for no good reason
Except that fallen stones and cracks
Bulging with weed suit my mood
Which is gloomy, irascible, selfish, among the split timbers
Of somebody's home, and the bleached rags of wallpaper.
My trouser-legs pied with water drops,
I knock a sparkling rain from hemlock-polls,
I crash a puddle up my shin,
Brush a nettle across my hand,
And swear—then sweat from what I said:
Indeed, the sun withdraws as if I stung.

Indeed, *she* withdrew as if I stung,
And I walk up and down among these canted beams,
     bricks and scraps,
Bitten walls and weed-stuffed gaps
Looking as it would feel now, if I walked back,
Across the carpets of my home, my own home.

PETER REDGROVE

The Early Purges

I was six when I first saw kittens drown.
Dan Taggart pitched them, "the scraggy wee shits",
Into a bucket; a frail metal sound,

Soft paws scraping like mad. But their tiny din
Was soon soused. They were slung on the snout
Of the pump and the water pumped in.

"Sure isn't it better for them now?" Dan said.
Like wet gloves they bobbed and shone till he sluiced
Them out on the dunghill, glossy and dead.

Suddenly frightened, for days I sadly hung
Round the yard, watching the three sogged remains
Turn mealy and crisp as old summer dung

Until I forgot them. But the fear came back
When Dan trapped big rats, snared rabbits, shot crows
Or, with a sickening tug, pulled old hens' necks.

Still, living displaces false sentiments
And now, when shrill pups are prodded to drown
I just shrug, "Bloody pups". It makes sense:

"Prevention of cruelty" talk cuts ice in town
Where they consider death unnatural,
But on well-run farms pests have to be kept down.

SEAMUS HEANEY

Genealogy

I was the dweller in the long cave
Of darkness, lining it with the forms
Of bulls. My hand matured early,

But turned to violence: I was the man
Watching later at the grim ford,
Armed with resentment; the quick stream

Remembers at sunset the raw crime.
The deed pursued me; I was the king
At the church keyhole, who saw death

Loping towards me. From that same hour
I fought for right, with the proud chiefs
Setting my name to the broad treaties.

I marched to Bosworth with the Welsh lords
To victory, but regretted after
The white house at the wood's heart.

I was the stranger in the new town,
Whose purse of tears was soon spent;
I filled it with a solider coin

At the dark sources. I stand now
In the hard light of the brief day
Without roots, but with many branches.

R. S. THOMAS

I May, I Might, I Must

If you will tell me why the fen
appears impassable, I then
will tell you why I think that I
can get across it if I try.

MARIANNE MOORE

Brush-Fire

In a city of small pleasures,
    small spoils, small powers,
The wooden shacks are largely burning.
Bodies of small people lie along the shabby streets,
An old palace is smouldering.
Wheeling bicycles piled with small bundles,
Families stream away, from north to south,
From south to north.

Who are these who are fighting those,
Fellow countrymen if not fellow men?
Some follow Prince X, some General Y.
Does Prince X lead the nobility,
And General Y the military?
Prince X is not particularly noble,
General Y is not so very military.
Some follow the Prince, for name's sake,
Or family's, or because he is there.
Some follow the General, for last month's pay,
Or family's sake, or because he walks in front.

56

Princes and generals have moderate ambitions.
An air-conditioned palace, a smarter G.H.Q.,
An Armstrong-Siddeley, another little wife.
The families, driven by some curious small ambition,
Stream away, from east to west, from west to east.
It is in their blood, to stream.
They know what is happening. None of them asks why—
They see that foreign tanks are running off with native drivers,
Foreign howitzers are manning native gunners—
As they pass by burning houses, on their way to burning
    houses.
Among such small people, the foreign shells
Make ridiculously big noises.

D. J. ENRIGHT

The Dance

In Breughel's great picture, The Kermess,
the dancers go round, they go round and
around, the squeal and the blare and the
tweedle of bagpipes, a bugle and fiddles
tipping their bellies (round as the thick-
sided glasses whose wash they impound)
their hips and their bellies off balance
to turn them. Kicking and rolling about
the Fair Grounds, swinging their butts, those
shanks must be sound to bear up under such
rollicking measures, prance as they dance
in Breughel's great picture, the Kermess.

WILLIAM CARLOS WILLIAMS

Horses on the Camargue

In the grey wastes of dread,
The haunt of shattered gulls where nothing moves
But in a shroud of silence like the dead,
I heard a sudden harmony of hooves,
And, turning, saw afar
A hundred snowy horses unconfined,
The silver runaways of Neptune's car
Racing, spray-curled, like waves before the wind.
Sons of the Mistral, fleet
As him with whose strong gusts they love to flee,
Who shod the flying thunders on their feet
And plunged them with the snortings of the sea;
Theirs is no earthly breed
Who only haunt the verges of the earth
And only on the sea's salt herbage feed—
Surely the great white breakers gave them birth.
For when for years a slave,
A horse of the Camargue, in alien lands,
Should catch some far-off fragrance of the wave
Carried far inland from his native sands,
Many have told the tale
Of how in fury, foaming at the rein,
He hurls his rider; and with lifted tail,
With coal-red eyes and cataracting mane,
Heading his course for home,
Though sixty foreign leagues before him sweep,
Will never rest until he breathes the foam
And hears the native thunder of the deep.
But when the great gusts rise
And lash their anger on these arid coasts,
When the scared gulls career with mournful cries
And whirl across the waste like driven ghosts:
When hail and fire converge,
The only souls to which they strike no pain

Are the white-crested fillies of the surge
And the white horses of the windy plain.
Then in their strength and pride
The stallions of the wilderness rejoice;
They feel their Master's trident in their side,
And high and shrill they answer to his voice.
With white tails smoking free,
Long streaming manes, and arching necks, they show
Their kinship to their sisters of the sea—
And forward hurl their thunderbolts of snow.
Still out of hardship bred,
Spirits of power and beauty and delight
Have ever on such frugal pastures fed
And loved to course with tempests through the night.

ROY CAMPBELL

Black Jackets

In the silence that prolongs the span
Rawly of music when the record ends,
    The red-haired boy who drove a van
In weekday overalls but, like his friends,

    Wore cycle boots and jacket here
To suit the Sunday hangout he was in,
    Heard, as he stretched back from his beer,
Leather creak softly round his neck and chin.

Before him, on a coal-black sleeve
Remote exertion had lined, scratched, and burned
    Insignia that could not revive
The heroic fall or climb where they were earned.

    On the other drinkers bent together,
Concocting selves for their impervious kit,
    He saw it as no more than leather
Which, taut across the shoulders grown to it,

    Sent through the dimness of a bar
As sudden and anonymous hints of light
    As those that shipping give, that are
Now flickers in the Bay, now lost in night.

    He stretched out like a cat, and rolled
The bitterish taste of beer upon his tongue,
    And listened to a joke being told:
The present was the things he stayed among.

    If it was only loss he wore,
He wore it to assert, with fierce devotion,
    Complicity and nothing more.
He recollected his initiation,

And one especially of the rites.
For on his shoulders they had put tattoos:
    The group's name on the left, The Knights,
And on the right the slogan Born to Lose.

THOM GUNN

Walking Away

It is eighteen years ago, almost to the day—
A sunny day with the leaves just turning,
The touch-lines new-ruled—since I watched you play
Your first game of football, then, like a satellite
Wrenched from its orbit, go drifting away

Behind a scatter of boys. I can see
You walking away from me towards the school
With the pathos of a half-fledged thing set free
Into a wilderness, the gait of one
Who finds no path where the path should be.

That hesitant figure, eddying away
Like a winged seed loosened from its parent stem,
Has something I never quite grasp to convey
About nature's give-and-take—the small, the scorching
Ordeals which fire one's irresolute clay.

I have had worse partings, but none that so
Gnaws at my mind still. Perhaps it is roughly
Saying what God alone could perfectly show—
How selfhood begins with a walking away,
And love is proved in the letting go.

C. DAY LEWIS

First Death

It is terrible and wonderful: we wake in the strange night
And there is one bed empty and one room full: tears fall,
The children comfort each other, hugging their knees,
       for what will the future be now, poor things?

And next day there is no school, and meals are disorderly,
Things bought from shops, not the old familiar dishes.
New uncles come from far away, soft-voiced strangers
Drinking extraordinary wines. A kind of abstract kindliness
Fills the house, and a smell of flowers. Impossible to be bad—

Other nights pass, under conceded night-lights and a cloud
Of questions: shall we ever go back to school? Ever again
Go to the pictures? Are we too poor for new shoes? Must
    we move
To a council house? Will any of our friends remember us?
Will it always be kind and quiet and sad, like this?

Uncles depart. We go for a week to a country aunt,
Then take a lodger. New shoes are bought—Oh,
       so this is the future!
How long will it last, this time? Never feel safe now.

D. J. ENRIGHT

Strange Meeting

It seemed that out of battle I escaped
Down some profound dull tunnel, long since scooped
Through granites which titanic wars had groined.
Yet also there encumbered sleepers groaned,
Too fast in thought or death to be bestirred.
Then, as I probed them, one sprang up, and stared
With piteous recognition in fixed eyes,
Lifting distressful hands as if to bless.
And by his smile, I knew that sullen hall,
By his dead smile I knew we stood in Hell.
With a thousand pains that vision's face was grained;
Yet no blood reached there from the upper ground,
And no guns thumped, or down the flues made moan.
"Strange friend," I said, "here is no cause to mourn."
"None," said that other, "save the undone years,
The hopelessness. Whatever hope is yours,
Was my life also; I went hunting wild
After the wildest beauty in the world,
Which lies not calm in eyes, or braided hair,
But mocks the steady running of the hour,
And if it grieves, grieves richlier than here.
For of my glee might many men have laughed,
And of my weeping something had been left,
Which must die now. I mean the truth untold,
The pity of war, the pity war distilled.
Now men will go content with what we spoiled,
Or, discontent, boil bloody, and be spilled.
They will be swift with swiftness of the tigress.
None will break ranks, though nations trek from progress.
Courage was mine, and I had mystery,
Wisdom was mine, and I had mastery:
To miss the march of this retreating world
Into vain citadels that are not walled.
Then, when much blood had clogged their chariot-wheels,

I would go up and wash them from sweet wells,
Even with truths that lie too deep for taint.
I would have poured my spirit without stint
But not through wounds; not on the cess of war.
Foreheads of men have bled where no wounds were.
I am the enemy you killed, my friend.
I knew you in this dark: for so you frowned
Yesterday through me as you jabbed and killed.
I parried; but my hands were loath and cold.
Let us sleep now. . .''

WILFRED OWEN

Bagpipe Music

It's no go the merrygoround, it's no go the rickshaw,
All we want is a limousine and a ticket for the peepshow,
Their knickers are made of crêpe-de-Chine, their shoes are
    made of python,
Their halls are lined with tiger-rugs and their walls with
    heads of bison.

John MacDonald found a corpse, put it under the sofa,
Waited till it came to life and hit it with a poker,
Sold its eyes for souvenirs, sold its blood for whisky,
Kept its bones for dumb-bells to use when he was fifty.

It's no go the Yogi-Man, it's no go Blavatsky,
All we want is a bank balance and a bit of skirt in a taxi.

Annie MacDougall went to milk, caught her foot in the heather,
Woke to hear a dance record playing of Old Vienna.
It's no go your maidenheads, it's no go your culture,
All we want is a Dunlop tyre and the devil mend the puncture.

The Laird o' Phelps spent Hogmanay declaring he was sober,
Counted his feet to prove the fact and found he had one foot
over.
Mrs Carmichael had her fifth, looked at the job with
repulsion,
Said to the midwife "Take it away; I'm through with over-
production."

It's no go the gossip column, it's no go the ceilidh,
All we want is a mother's help and a sugar-stick for the baby.

Willie Murray cut his thumb, couldn't count the damage,
Took the hide of an Ayrshire cow and used it for a bandage.
His brother caught three hundred cran when the seas were
lavish,
Threw the bleeders back in the sea and went upon the parish.

It's no go the Herring Board, it's no go the Bible,
All we want is a packet of fags when our hands are idle.

It's no go the picture palace, it's no go the stadium,
It's no go the country cot with a pot of pink geraniums,
It's no go the Government grants, it's no go the elections,
Sit on your arse for fifty years and hang your hat on a pension.

It's no go my honey love, it's no go my poppet;
Work your hands from day to day, the winds will blow the
profit.
The glass is falling hour by hour, the glass will fall for ever;
But if you break the bloody glass you won't hold up the
weather.

LOUIS MACNEICE

Lore

Job Davies, eighty-five
Winters old, and still alive
With the slow poison
And treachery of the seasons.

Miserable? Kick my arse!
It needs more than the rain's hearse,
Wind-drawn, to pull me off
The great perch of my laugh.

What's living but courage?
Paunch full of hot porridge,
Nerves strengthened with tea,
Peat-black, dawn found me

Mowing where the grass grew,
Bearded with golden dew.
Rhythm of the long scythe
Kept this tall frame lithe.

What to do? Stay green.
Never mind the machine,
Whose fuel is human souls.
Live large, man, and dream small.

R. S. Thomas

The Map

Land lies in water; it is shadowed green.
Shadows, or are they shallows, at its edges
showing the line of long sea-weeded ledges
where weeds hang to the simple blue from green.
Or does the land lean down to lift the sea from under,
drawing it unperturbed around itself?
Along the fine tan sandy shelf
is the land tugging at the sea from under?

The shadow of Newfoundland lies flat and still.
Labrador's yellow, where the moony Eskimo
has oiled it. We can stroke these lovely bays,
under a glass as if they were expected to blossom,
or as if to provide a clean cage for invisible fish.
The names of seashore towns run out to sea,
the names of cities cross the neighbouring mountains
—the printer here experiencing the same excitement
as when emotion too far exceeds its cause.
These peninsulas take the water between thumb and finger
like women feeling for the smoothness of yard-goods.

Mapped waters are more quiet than the land is,
lending the land their waves' own conformation:
and Norway's hare runs south in agitation,
profiles investigate the sea, where land is.
Are they assigned, or can the countries pick their colours?
—What suits the character or the native waters best.
Topography displays no favorites; North's as near as West.
More delicate than the historians' are the map-makers' colours.

ELIZABETH BISHOP

from *Northumbrian Sequence*

Let in the wind
Let in the rain
Let in the moors tonight,

The storm beats on my window-pane,
Night stands at my bed-foot,
Let in the fear,
Let in the pain,
Let in the trees that toss and groan,
Let in the north tonight.

Let in the nameless formless power
That beats upon my door,
Let in the ice, let in the snow,
The banshee howling on the moor,
The bracken-bush on the bleak hillside,
Let in the dead tonight.

The whistling ghost behind the dyke,
The dead that rot in mire,
Let in the thronging ancestors
The unfulfilled desire,
Let in the wraith of the dead earl,
Let in the unborn tonight.

Let in the cold,
Let in the wet,
Let in the loneliness,
Let in the quick,
Let in the dead,
Let in the unpeopled skies.

Oh how can virgin fingers weave
A covering for the void,
How can my fearful heart conceive
Gigantic solitude?
How can a house so small contain
A company so great?
Let in the dark,
Let in the dead,
Let in your love tonight.

Let in the snow that numbs the grave,
Let in the acorn-tree,
The mountain stream and mountain stone,
Let in the bitter sea.

Fearful is my virgin heart
And frail my virgin form,
And must I then take pity on
The raging of the storm
That rose up from the great abyss
Before the earth was made,
That pours the stars in cataracts
And shakes this violent world?

Let in the fire,
Let in the power,
Let in the invading might.

Gentle must my fingers be
And pitiful my heart
Since I must bind in human form
A living power so great,
A living impulse great and wild
That cries about my house
With all the violence of desire
Desiring this my peace.

Pitiful my heart must hold
The lonely stars at rest,
Have pity on the raven's cry
The torrent and the eagle's wing,
The icy water of the tarn
And on the biting blast.

Let in the wound,
Let in the pain,
Let in your child tonight.

KATHLEEN RAINE

In Westminster Abbey

Let me take this other glove off
    As the *vox humana* swells,
And the beauteous fields of Eden
    Bask beneath the Abbey bells.
Here, where England's statesmen lie,
Listen to a lady's cry.

Gracious Lord, oh bomb the Germans.
    Spare their women for Thy Sake,
And if that is not too easy
    We will pardon Thy Mistake.
But, gracious Lord, whate'er shall be,
Don't let anyone bomb me.

Keep our Empire undismembered
    Guide our Forces by Thy Hand,
Gallant blacks from far Jamaica,
    Honduras and Togoland;
Protect them Lord in all their fights,
And, even more, protect the whites.

70

Think of what our Nation stands for,
    Books from Boots' and country lanes,
Free speech, free passes, class distinction,
    Democracy and proper drains.
Lord, put beneath Thy special care
One-eighty-nine Cadogan Square.

Although dear Lord I am a sinner,
    I have done no major crime;
Now I'll come to Evening Service
    Whensoever I have the time.
So, Lord, reserve for me a crown,
And do not let my shares go down.

I will labour for Thy Kingdom,
    Help our lads to win the war,
Send white feathers to the cowards
    Join the Women's Army Corps,
Then wash the Steps around Thy Throne
In the Eternal Safety Zone.

Now I feel a little better,
    What a treat to hear Thy Word,
Where the bones of leading statesmen,
    Have so often been interr'd.
And now, dear Lord, I cannot wait
Because I have a luncheon date.

JOHN BETJEMAN

The Love Song of J. Alfred Prufrock

S'io credesse che mia risposta fosse
A persona che mai tornasse al mondo,
Questa fiamma staria senza piu scosse.
Ma perciocche giammai di questo fondo
Non torno vivo alcun, s'i'odo il vero,
Senza tema d'infamia ti rispondo.

Let us go then, you and I,
When the evening is spread out against the sky
Like a patient etherised upon a table;
Let us go, through certain half-deserted streets,
The muttering retreats
Of restless nights in one-night cheap hotels
And sawdust restaurants with oyster-shells:
Streets that follow like a tedious argument
Of insidious intent
To lead you to an overwhelming question . . .
Oh, do not ask, "What is it?"
Let us go and make our visit.

In the room the women come and go
Talking of Michelangelo.

The yellow fog that rubs its back upon the window-panes,
The yellow smoke that rubs its muzzle on the window-panes
Licked its tongue into the corners of the evening,
Lingered upon the pools that stand in drains,
Let fall upon its back the soot that falls from chimneys,
Slipped by the terrace, made a sudden leap,
And seeing that it was a soft October night,
Curled once about the house, and fell asleep.

And indeed there will be time
For the yellow smoke that slides along the street
Rubbing its back upon the window-panes;
There will be time, there will be time
To prepare a face to meet the faces that you meet;
There will be time to murder and create,
And time for all the works and days of hands
That lift and drop a question on your plate;
Time for you and time for me,
And time yet for a hundred indecisions,
And for a hundred visions and revisions,
Before the taking of a toast and tea.

In the room the women come and go
Talking of Michelangelo.

And indeed there will be time
To wonder, "Do I dare?" and, "Do I dare?"
Time to turn back and descend the stair,
With a bald spot in the middle of my hair—
(They will say: "How his hair is growing thin!")
My morning coat, my collar mounting firmly to the chin,
My necktie rich and modest, but asserted by a simple pin—
(They will say: "But how his arms and legs are thin!")
Do I dare
Disturb the universe?
In a minute there is time
For decisions and revisions which a minute will reverse.

For I have known them all already, known them all—
Have known the evenings, mornings, afternoons,
I have measured out my life with coffee spoons;
I know the voices dying with a dying fall
Beneath the music from a farther room.
So how should I presume?

And I have known the eyes already, known them all—
The eyes that fix you in a formulated phrase,
And when I am formulated, sprawling on a pin,
When I am pinned and wriggling on the wall,
Then how should I begin
To spit out all the butt-ends of my days and ways?
      And how should I presume?

And I have known the arms already, known them all—
Arms that are braceleted and white and bare
(But in the lamplight, downed with light brown hair!)
Is it perfume from a dress
That makes me so digress?
Arms that lie along a table, or wrap about a shawl.
      And should I then presume?
      And how should I begin?

        .   .   .   .   .

Shall I say, I have gone at dusk through narrow streets
And watched the smoke that rises from the pipes
Of lonely men in shirt-sleeves, leaning out of windows? . . .

I should have been a pair of ragged claws
Scuttling across the floors of silent seas.

        .   .   .   .   .   .

And the afternoon, the evening, sleeps so peacefully!
Smoothed by long fingers,
Asleep . . . tired . . . or it malingers,
Stretched on the floor, here beside you and me.
Should I, after tea and cakes and ices,
Have the strength to force the moment to its crisis?
But though I have wept and fasted, wept and prayed,

Though I have seen my head (grown slightly bald)
    brought in upon a platter,
I am no prophet—and here's no great matter;
I have seen the moment of my greatness flicker,
And I have seen the eternal Footman hold my coat, and
    snicker,
And in short, I was afraid.

And would it have been worth it, after all,
After the cups, the marmalade, the tea,
Among the porcelain, among some talk of you and me,
Would it have been worth while,
To have bitten off the matter with a smile,
To have squeezed the universe into a ball
To roll it toward some overwhelming question,
To say: "I am Lazarus, come from the dead,
Come back to tell you all, I shall tell you all"—
If one, settling a pillow by her head,
        Should say: "That is not what I meant at all.
        That is not it, at all."

And would it have been worth it, after all,
Would it have been worth while,
After the sunsets and the dooryards and the sprinkled
    streets,
After the novels, after the teacups, after the skirts that
    trail along the floor—
And this, and so much more?—
It is impossible to say just what I mean!
But as if a magic lantern threw the nerves in patterns on
    a screen:
Would it have been worth while
If one, settling a pillow or throwing off a shawl,
And turning toward the window, should say:
        "That is not it at all,
        That is not what I meant, at all."

        .   .   .   .

No! I am not Prince Hamlet, nor was meant to be;
Am an attendant lord, one that will do
To swell a progress, start a scene or two,
Advise the prince; no doubt, an easy tool,
Deferential, glad to be of use,
Politic, cautious, and meticulous;
Full of high sentence, but a bit obtuse;
At times, indeed, almost ridiculous—
Almost, at times, the Fool.

I grow old . . . I grow old . . .
I shall wear the bottoms of my trousers rolled.

Shall I part my hair behind? Do I dare to eat a peach?
I shall wear white flannel trousers, and walk upon the beach.
I have heard the mermaids singing, each to each.

I do not think that they will sing to me.

I have seen them riding seaward on the waves
Combing the white hair of the waves blown back
When the wind blows the water white and black.

We have lingered in the chambers of the sea
By sea-girls wreathed with seaweed red and brown
Till human voices wake us, and we drown.

                                                    T. S. Eliot

The Garden

En robe de parade
SAMAIN

Like a skein of loose silk blown against a wall
She walks by the railing of a path in Kensington Gardens,
And she is dying piece-meal
     of a sort of emotional anaemia.

And round about there is a rabble
Of the filthy, sturdy, unkillable infants of the very poor.
They shall inherit the earth.

In her is the end of breeding.
Her boredom is exquisite and excessive.
She would like some one to speak to her,
And is almost afraid that I
     will commit that indiscretion.

EZRA POUND

On This Island

Look, stranger, on this island now
The leaping light for your delight discovers,
Stand stable here
And silent be,
That through the channels of the ear
May wander like a river
The swaying sound of the sea.

Here at the small field's ending pause
When the chalk wall falls to the foam and its tall ledges
Oppose the pluck
And knock of the tide,
And the shingle scrambles after the suck-
ing surf,
And the gull lodges
A moment on its sheer side.

Far off like floating seed the ships
Diverge on urgent voluntary errands,
And the full view
Indeed may enter
And move in memory as now these clouds do,
That pass the harbour mirror
And all the summer through the water saunter.

W. H. AUDEN

Two Look at Two

Love and forgetting might have carried them
A little further up the mountainside
With night so near, but not much further up.
They must have halted soon in any case
With thoughts of the path back, how rough it was
With rock and washout, and unsafe in darkness;
When they were halted by a tumbled wall
With barbed-wire binding. They stood facing this,
Spending what onward impulse they still had
In one last look the way they must not go,
On up the failing path, where, if a stone
Or earthslide moved at night, it moved itself;
No footstep moved it. "This is all," they sighed,
"Good-night to woods." But not so; there was more.
A doe from round a spruce stood looking at them
Across the wall, as near the wall as they.
She saw them in their field, they her in hers.
The difficulty of seeing what stood still,
Like some up-ended boulder split in two,
Was in her clouded eyes: they saw no fear there.
She seemed to think that two thus they were safe.
Then, as if they were something that, though strange,
She could not trouble her mind with too long,
She sighed and passed unscared along the wall.
"*This*, then, is all. What more is there to ask?"
But no, not yet. A snort to bid them wait.
A buck from round the spruce stood looking at them
Across the wall as near the wall as they.
This was an antlered buck of lusty nostril,
Not the same doe come back into her place.
He viewed them quizzically with jerks of head,
As if to ask, "Why don't you make some motion?
Or give some sign of life? Because you can't.
I doubt if you're as living as you look."

Thus till he had them almost feeling dared
To stretch a proffering hand—and a spell-breaking.
Then he too passed unscared along the wall.
Two had seen two, whichever side you spoke from.
"This *must* be all." It was all. Still they stood,
A great wave from it going over them,
As if the earth in one unlooked-for favor
Had made them certain earth returned their love.

ROBERT FROST

The Dove-Breeder

Love struck into his life
Like a hawk into a dovecote.
What a cry went up!
Every gentle pedigree dove
Blindly clattered and beat,
And the mild-mannered dove-breeder
Shrieked at that raider.

He might well wring his hands
And let his tears drop:
He will win no more prizes
With fantails or pouters,
(After all these years
Through third, up through second places
Till they were all world beaters . . .)

Yet he soon dried his tears

Now he rides the morning mist
With a big-eyed hawk on his fist.

TED HUGHES

Circus Lion

Lumbering haunches, pussyfoot tread, a pride of
Lions under the arcs
Walk in, leap up, sit pedestalled there and glum
As a row of Dickensian clerks.

Their eyes are slag. Only a muscle flickering,
A bored, theatrical roar
Witness now to the furnaces that drove them
Exultant along the spoor.

In preyward, elastic leap they are sent through paper
Hoops at another's will
And a whip's crack: afterwards, in their cages,
They tear the provided kill.

Caught young, can this public animal ever dream of
Stars, distances and thunders?
Does he twitch in sleep for ticks, dried water-holes,
Rogue elephants, or hunters?

Sawdust, not burning desert, is the ground
Of his to-fro, to-fro pacing,
Barred with the zebra shadows that imply
Sun's free wheel, man's coercing.

See this abdicated beast, once king
Of them all, nibble his claws:
Not anger enough left—no, nor despair—
To break his teeth on the bars.

C. Day Lewis

The Bonnie Broukit Bairn

crimson

Mars is braw in crammasy,
Venus in a green silk goun,

golden

The auld mune shak's her gowden feathers,

pack of nonsense

Their starry talk's a wheen o' blethers,
Nane for thee a thochtie sparin',

pale-faced child

Earth, thou bonnie broukit bairn!

weep

—*But greet, an' in your tears ye'll droun*

collection

The haill clanjamfrie!

HUGH MACDIARMID

Ballad of the Bread Man

Mary stood in the kitchen
Baking a loaf of bread.
An angel flew in through the window.
We've a job for you, he said.

God in his big gold heaven,
Sitting in his big blue chair,
Wanted a mother for his little son.
Suddenly saw you there.

Mary shook and trembled,
It isn't true what you say.
Don't say that, said the angel.
The baby's on its way.

Joseph was in the workshop
Planing a piece of wood.
The old man's past it, the neighbours said.
That girl's been up to no good.

And who was that elegant feller,
They said, in the shiny gear?
The things they said about Gabriel
Were hardly fit to hear.

Mary never answered,
Mary never replied.
She kept the information,
Like the baby, safe inside.

It was election winter.
They went to vote in town.
When Mary found her time had come
The hotels let her down.

The baby was born in an annex
Next to the local pub.
At midnight, a delegation
Turned up from the Farmers' Club.

They talked about an explosion
That cracked a hole in the sky,
Said they'd been sent to the Lamb & Flag
To see god come down from on high.

A few days later a bishop
And a five-star general were seen
With the head of an African country
In a bullet-proof limousine.

We've come, they said, with tokens
For the little boy to choose.
Told the tale about war and peace
In the television news.

After them came the soldiers
With rifle and bomb and gun,
Looking for enemies of the state.
The family had packed and gone.

When they got back to the village
The neighbours said, to a man,
That boy will never be one of us,
Though he does what he blessed well can.

He went round to all the people
A paper crown on his head.
Here is some bread from my father.
Take, eat, he said.

Nobody seemed very hungry.
Nobody seemed to care.
Nobody saw the god in himself
Quietly standing there.

He finished up in the papers.
He came to a very bad end.
He was charged with bringing the living to life.
No man was that prisoner's friend.

There's only one kind of punishment
To fit that kind of a crime.
They rigged a trial and shot him dead.
They were only just in time.

They lifted the young man by the leg,
They lifted him by the arm,
They locked him in a cathedral
In case he came to harm.

They stored him safe as water
Under seven rocks.
One Sunday morning he burst out
Like a jack-in-the-box.

Through the town he went walking.
He showed them the holes in his head.
Now do you want any loaves? he cried.
Not today, they said.

CHARLES CAUSLEY

The Disquieting Muses

Mother, mother, what illbred aunt
Or what disfigured and unsightly
Cousin did you so unwisely keep
Unasked to my christening, that she
Sent these ladies in her stead
With heads like darning-eggs to nod
And nod and nod at foot and head
And at the left side of my crib?

Mother, who made to order stories
Of Mixie Blackshort the heroic bear,
Mother, whose witches always, always
Got baked into gingerbread, I wonder
Whether you saw them, whether you said
Words to rid me of those three ladies
Nodding by night around my bed,
Mouthless, eyeless, with stitched bald head.

In the hurricane, when father's twelve
Study windows bellied in
Like bubbles about to break, you fed
My brother and me cookies and ovaltine
And helped the two of us to choir:
"Thor is angry: boom boom boom!
Thor is angry: we don't care!"
But these ladies broke the panes.

When on tiptoe the schoolgirls danced,
Blinking flashlights like fireflies
And singing the glowworm song, I could
Not lift a foot in the twinkle-dress
But, heavy-footed, stood aside
In the shadow cast by my dismal-headed
Godmothers, and you cried and cried:
And the shadow stretched, the lights went out.

Mother, you sent me to piano lessons
And praised my arabesques and trills
Although each teacher found my touch
Oddly wooden in spite of scales
And the hours of practising, my ear
Tone-deaf and yes, unteachable.
I learned, I learned, I learned elsewhere,
From muses unhired by you, dear mother.

I woke one day to see you, mother,
Floating above me in bluest air
On a green balloon bright with a million
Flowers and bluebirds that never were
Never, never, found anywhere.
But the little planet bobbed away
Like a soap-bubble as you called: Come here!
And I faced my travelling companions.

Day now, night now, at head, side, feet,
They stand their vigil in gowns of stone,
Faces blank as the day I was born,
Their shadows long in the setting sun
That never brightens or goes down.
And this is the kingdom you bore me to,
Mother, mother. But no frown of mine
Will betray the company I keep.

SYLVIA PLATH

Futility

Move him into the sun—
Gently its touch awoke him once,
At home, whispering of fields unsown.
Always it woke him, even in France,
Until this morning and this snow.
If anything might rouse him now
The kind old sun will know.

Think how it wakes the seeds,—
Woke, once, the clays of a cold star.
Are limbs, so dear-achieved, are sides,
Full-nerved—still warm—too hard to stir?
Was it for this the clay grew tall?
—O what made fatuous sunbeams toil
To break earth's sleep at all?

WILFRED OWEN

My Father in the Night Commanding No

My father in the night commanding No
Has work to do. Smoke issues from his lips;
    He reads in silence.
The frogs are croaking and the streetlamps glow.

And then my mother winds the gramophone;
The Bride of Lammermoor begins to shriek—
    Or reads a story
About a prince, a castle, and a dragon.

The moon is glittering above the hill.
I stand before the gateposts of the King—
    So runs the story—
Of Thule, at midnight when the mice are still.

And I have been in Thule! It has come true—
The journey and the danger of the world,
    All that there is
To bear and to enjoy, endure and do.

Landscapes, seascapes . . . where have I been led?
The names of cities—Paris, Venice, Rome—
    Held out their arms.
A feathered god, seductive, went ahead.

Here is my house. Under a red rose tree
A child is swinging; another gravely plays.
    They are not surprised
That I am here; they were expecting me.

And yet my father sits and reads in silence,
My mother sheds a tear, the moon is still,
    And the dark wind
Is murmuring that nothing ever happens.

Beyond his jurisdiction as I move
Do I not prove him wrong? And yet, it's true
    They will not change
There, on the stage of terror and of love.

The actors in that playhouse always sit
In fixed positions—father, mother, child
    With painted eyes.
How sad it is to be a little puppet!

Their heads are wooden. And you once pretended
To understand them! Shake them as you will,
    They cannot speak.
Do what you will, the comedy is ended.

Father, why did you work? Why did you weep,
Mother? Was the story so important?
    "Listen!" the wind
Said to the children, and they fell asleep.

LOUIS SIMPSON

Jesus and His Mother

My only son, more God's than mine,
Stay in this garden ripe with pears.
The yielding of their substance wears
A modest and contented shine:
And when they weep with age, not brine
But lazy syrup are their tears.
"I am my own and not my own."

He seemed much like another man,
That silent foreigner who trod
Outside my door with lily rod:
How could I know what I began
Meeting the eyes more furious than
The eyes of Joseph, those of God?
I was my own and not my own.

And who are these twelve labouring men?
I do not understand your words:
I taught you speech, we named the birds,
You marked their big migrations then
Like any child. So turn again
To silence from the place of crowds.
"I am my own and not my own."

Why are you sullen when I speak?
Here are your tools, the saw and knife
And hammer on your bench. Your life
Is measured here in week and week
Planed as the furniture you make,
And I will teach you like a wife
To be my own and all my own.

Who like an arrogant wind blown
Where he may please, needs no content?
Yet I remember how you went
To speak with scholars in furred gown.
I hear an outcry in the town;
Who carried that dark instrument?
"One all his own and not his own."

Treading the green and nimble sward
I stare at a strange shadow thrown.
Are you the boy I bore alone,
No doctor near to cut the cord?
I cannot reach to call you Lord,
Answer me as my only son.
"I am my own and not my own."

THOM GUNN

Places, Loved Ones

No, I have never found
The place where I could say
This is my proper ground,
Here I shall stay;
Nor met that special one
Who has an instant claim
On everything I own
Down to my name;

To find such seems to prove
You want no choice in where
To build, or whom to love;
You ask them to bear
You off irrevocably,
So that it's not your fault
Should the town turn dreary,
The girl a dolt.

Yet, having missed them, you're
Bound, none the less, to act
As if what you settled for
Mashed you, in fact;
And wiser to keep away
From thinking you still might trace
Uncalled-for to this day
Your person, your place.

PHILIP LARKIN

No One Cares Less Than I

"No one cares less than I,
Nobody knows but God,
Whether I am destined to lie
Under a foreign clod,"
Were the words I made to the bugle call in the morning.

But laughing, storming, scorning,
Only the bugles know
What the bugles say in the morning,
And they do not care, when they blow
The call that I heard and made words to early this morning.

EDWARD THOMAS

Bavarian Gentians

Not every man has gentians in his house
In Soft September, at slow, sad Michaelmas.

Bavarian gentians, big and dark, only dark
darkening the day-time, torch-like with the smoking
  blueness of Pluto's gloom,
ribbed and torch-like, with their blaze of darkness spread
  blue
down flattening into points, flattened under the sweep of white
  day
torch-flower of the blue-smoking darkness, Pluto's dark-blue
  daze,
black lamps from the halls of Dis, burning dark blue,
giving off darkness, blue darkness, as Demeter's pale lamps
  give off light,
lead me then, lead the way.

Reach me a gentian, give me a torch!
let me guide myself with the blue, forked torch of this flower
down the darker and darker stairs, where blue is darkened on
  blueness
even where Persephone goes, just now, from the frosted
  September
to the sightless realm where darkness is awake upon the dark
and Persephone herself is but a voice
or a darkness invisible enfolded in the deeper dark
of the arms Plutonic, and pierced with the passion of dense
  gloom,
among the splendour of torches of darkness, shedding
  darkness on the lost bride and her groom.

D. H. Lawrence

Song of a Man Who Has Come Through

Not I, not I, but the wind that blows through me!
A fine wind is blowing the new direction of Time.
If only I let it bear me, carry me, if only it carry me!
If only I am sensitive, subtle, oh, delicate, a winged gift!
If only, most lovely of all, I yield myself and am borrowed
By the fine, fine wind that takes its course through the
    chaos of the world
Like a fine, an exquisite chisel, a wedge-blade inserted;
If only I am keen and hard like the sheer tip of a wedge
Driven by invisible blows,
The rock will split, we shall come at the wonder, we shall
    find the Hesperides.

Oh, for the wonder that bubbles into my soul,
I would be a good fountain, a good well-head,
Would blur no whisper, spoil no expression.

What is the knocking?
What is the knocking at the door in the night?
It is somebody wants to do us harm.

No, no, it is the three strange angels.
Admit them, admit them.

D. H. LAWRENCE

Fern Hill

Now as I was young and easy under the apple boughs
About the lilting house and happy as the grass was green,
    The night above the dingle starry,
       Time let me hail and climb
    Golden in the heydays of his eyes,
And honoured among wagons I was prince of the apple towns
And once below a time I lordly had the trees and leaves
       Trail with daisies and barley
    Down by the rivers of the windfall light.

And as I was green and carefree, famous among the barns
About the happy yard and singing as the farm was home,
    In the sun that is young once only,
       Time let me play and be
    Golden in the mercy of his means,
And green and golden I was huntsman and herdsman, the
    calves
Sang to my horn, the foxes on the hills barked clear and cold,
       And the sabbath rang slowly
    In the pebbles of the holy streams.

All the sun long it was running, it was lovely, the hay
Fields high as the house, the tunes from the chimneys, it
    was air
    And playing, lovely and watery
       And fire green as grass.
    And nightly under the simple stars
As I rode to sleep the owls were bearing the farm away,
All the moon long I heard, blessed among stables, the night-
    jars
       Flying with the ricks, and the horses
          Flashing into the dark.

And then to awake, and the farm, like a wanderer white
With the dew, come back, the cock on his shoulder: it was all
 Shining, it was Adam and maiden,
  The sky gathered again
 And the sun grew round that very day.
So it must have been after the birth of the simple light
In the first, spinning place, the spellbound horses walking
 warm
 Out of the whinnying green stable
  On to the fields of praise.

And honoured among foxes and pheasants by the gay house
Under the new made clouds and happy as the heart was long,
 In the sun born over and over,
  I ran my heedless ways,
 My wishes raced through the house high hay
And nothing I cared, at my sky-blue trades, that time allows
In all his tuneful turning so few and such morning songs
 Before the children green and golden
  Follow him out of grace,

Nothing I cared, in the lamb white days, that time would take
 me
Up to the swallow thronged loft by the shadow of my hand,
 In the moon that is always rising,
  Nor that riding to sleep
 I should hear him fly with the high fields
And wake to the farm forever fled from the childless land.
Oh as I was young and easy in the mercy of his means,
  Time held me green and dying
 Though I sang in my chains like the sea.

DYLAN THOMAS

Spinster

Now this particular girl
During a ceremonious April walk
With her latest suitor
Found herself, of a sudden, intolerably struck
By the birds' irregular babel
And the leaves' litter.

By this tumult afflicted, she
Observed her lover's gestures unbalance the air,
His gait stray uneven
Through a rank wilderness of fern and flower.
She judged petals in disarray
The whole season, sloven.

How she longed for winter then!—
Scrupulously austere in its order
Of white and black
Ice and rock, each sentiment within border,
And heart's frosty discipline
Exact as a snowflake.

But here—a burgeoning
Unruly enough to pitch her five queenly wits
Into vulgar motley—
A treason not to be borne. Let idiots
Reel giddy in bedlam spring:
She withdrew neatly.

And round her house she set
Such a barricade of barb and check
Against mutinous weather
As no mere insurgent man could hope to break
With curse, fist, threat
Or love, either.

SYLVIA PLATH

98

Salutation

O generation of the thoroughly smug
    and thoroughly uncomfortable,
I have seen fishermen picnicking in the sun,
I have seen them with untidy families,
I have seen their smiles full of teeth
    and heard ungainly laughter.
And I am happier than you are,
And they were happier than I am;
And the fish swim in the lake
    and do not even own clothing.

EZRA POUND

The Lake Isle

O God, O Venus, O Mercury, patron of thieves,
Give me in due time, I beseech you, a little tobacco-shop
With the little bright boxes
    piled up neatly upon the shelves
And the loose fragrant cavendish
    and the shag,
And the bright Virginia
    loose under the bright glass cases,
And a pair of scales not too greasy,
And the whores dropping in for a word or two in passing,
For a flip word, and to tidy their hair a bit.

O God, O Venus, O Mercury, patron of thieves,
Lend me a little tobacco-shop,
    or install me in any profession
Save this damn'd profession of writing,
    where one needs one's brains all the time.

EZRA POUND

Merlin

O Merlin in your crystal cave
Deep in the diamond of the day,
Will there ever be a singer
Whose music will smooth away
The furrow drawn by Adam's finger
Across the meadow and the wave?
Or a runner who'll outrun
Man's long shadow driving on,
Break through the gate of memory
And hang the apple on the tree?
Will your magic ever show
The sleeping bride shut in her bower,
The day wreathed in its mound of snow
And Time locked in his tower?

EDWIN MUIR

O Where are You Going?

"O where are you going?" said reader to rider,
"That valley is fatal when furnaces burn,
Yonder's the midden whose odours will madden,
That gap is the grave where the tall return."

"O do you imagine," said fearer to farer,
"That dusk will delay on your path to the pass,
Your diligent looking discover the lacking
Your footsteps feel from granite to grass?"

"O what was that bird" said horror to hearer,
"Did you see that shape in the twisted trees?
Behind you swiftly the figure comes softly,
The spot on your skin is a shocking disease."

"Out of this house"—said rider to reader,
"Yours never will"—said farer to fearer,
"They're looking for you"—said hearer to horror,
As he left them there, as he left them there.

W. H. AUDEN

Take One Home for the Kiddies

On shallow straw, in shadeless glass,
Huddled by empty bowls, they sleep:
No dark, no dam, no earth, no grass—
Mam, get us one of them to keep.

Living toys are something novel,
But it soon wears off somehow.
Fetch the shoebox, fetch the shovel—
Mam, we're playing funerals now.

PHILIP LARKIN

The Hawk

On Sunday the hawk fell on Bigging
  And a chicken screamed
  Lost in its own little snowstorm.
And on Monday he fell on the moor
  And the Field Club
  Raised a hundred silent prisms.
And on Tuesday he fell on the hill
  And the happy lamb
  Never knew why the loud collic straddled him.
And on Wednesday he fell on a bush
  And the blackbird
  Laid by his little flute for the last time.
And on Thursday he fell on Cleat
  And peerie Tom's rabbit
  Swung in a single arc from shore to hill.
And on Friday he fell on a ditch
  But the rampant rat,
  That eye and that tooth, quenched his flame.
And on Saturday he fell on Bigging
  And Jock lowered his gun
  And nailed a small wing over the corn.

GEORGE MACKAY BROWN

Fife Tune

(6/8) for Sixth Platoon, 308th I.T.C.

One morning in spring
We marched from Devizes
All shapes and all sizes
Like beads on a string,
But yet with a swing
We trod the bluemetal
And full of high fettle
We started to sing.

She ran down the stair
A twelve-year old darling
And laughing and calling
She tossed her bright hair;
Then silent to stare
At the men flowing past her—
There were all she could master
Adoring her there.

It's seldom I'll see
A sweeter or prettier;
I doubt we'll forget her
In two years or three,
And lucky he'll be
She takes for a lover
While we are far over
The treacherous sea.

JOHN MANIFOLD

Encounter With a God

Ono-no-komache the poetess
sat on the ground among her flowers,
sat in her delicate-patterned dress
thinking of the rowers,
thinking of the god Daikoku.

Thinking of the rock pool
and carp in the waterfall at night.
Daikoku in accordance with the rule
is beautiful, she said, with a slight
tendency to angles.

But Daikoku came
who had been drinking all night
with the greenish gods of chance and fame.
He was rotund standing in the moonlight,
with a round, white paunch.

Who said
I am not beautiful,
I do not wish to be wonderfully made,
I am not intoxicated, dutiful daughter,
and I will not be in a poem.

But the poetess sat still
holding her head and making verses:
"How intricate and peculiarly well-
arranged the symmetrical belly-purses
of Lord Daikoku."

KEITH DOUGLAS

A Summer Night

Out on the lawn I lie in bed,
Vega conspicuous overhead
    In the windless nights of June,
As congregated leaves complete
Their day's activity; my feet
    Point to the rising moon.

Lucky, this point in time and space
Is chosen as my working-place,
    Where the sexy airs of summer,
The bathing hours and the bare arms,
The leisured drives through a land of farms
    Are good to a newcomer.

Equal with colleagues in a ring
I sit on each calm evening
    Enchanted as the flowers
The opening light draws out of hiding
With all its gradual dove-like pleading,
    Its logic and its powers:

That later we, though parted then,
May still recall these evenings when
    Fear gave his watch no look;
The lion griefs loped from the shade
And on our knees their muzzles laid,
    And Death put down his book.

Now north and south and east and west
Those I love lie down to rest;
    The moon looks on them all,
The healers and the brilliant talkers
The eccentrics and the silent walkers,
    The dumpy and the tall.

She climbs the European sky,
Churches and power-stations lie
　　Alike among earth's fixtures:
Into the galleries she peers
And blankly as a butcher stares
　　Upon the marvellous pictures.

To gravity attentive, she
Can notice nothing here, though we
　　Whom hunger does not move,
From gardens where we feel secure
Look up and with a sigh endure
　　The tyrannies of love:

And, gentle, do not care to know,
Where Poland draws her eastern bow,
　　What violence is done,
Nor ask what doubtful act allows
Our freedom in this English house,
　　Our picnics in the sun.

Soon, soon, through dykes of our content
The crumpling flood will force a rent
　　And, taller than a tree,
Hold sudden death before our eyes
Whose river dreams long hid the size
　　And vigours of the sea.

But when the waters make retreat
And through the black mud first the wheat
　　In shy green stalks appears,
When stranded monsters gasping lie,
And sounds of riveting terrify
　　Their whorled unsubtle ears,

May these delights we dread to lose,
This privacy, need no excuse
   But to that strength belong,
As through a child's rash happy cries
The drowned parental voices rise
   In unlamenting song.

After discharges of alarm
All unpredicted let them calm
   The pulse of nervous nations,
Forgive the murderer in his glass,
Tough in their patience to surpass
   The tigress her swift motions.

W. H. AUDEN

The Next War

War's a joke for me and you,
While we know such dreams are true.

Out there, we've walked quite friendly up to Death;
    Sat down and eaten with him, cool and bland,—
    Pardoned his spilling mess-tins in our hand.
We've sniffed the green thick odour of his breath,—
Our eyes wept, but our courage didn't writhe.
    He's spat at us with bullets and he's coughed
    Shrapnel. We chorussed when he sang aloft;
We whistled while he shaved us with his scythe.

Oh, Death was never enemy of ours!
    We laughed at him, we leagued with him, old chum.
No soldier's paid to kick against his powers
    We laughed, knowing that better men would come,
And greater wars; when each proud fighter brags
He wars on Death—for lives; not men—for flags.

WILFRED OWEN

Hoot Owls

Owls that cry in the night,
(I have noted towards dawn)
Hooting in call and in answer,
Were supposed to be mysterious;
Indeed, their voice is enchanting,
With a far-away roll and fall,
Yet imagine my distrust
Of what used to be poetical
To learn that these dull birds,
Instead of leading us on
Into labyrinthian melancholy,
Actually make their hoots
To petrify, as it were,
And scare stiff small animals,
Who, thus mesmerized,
Cannot move for deadly fear,
Whereupon the hungry hoot owls
Wing down swiftly, killing
Their prey in handsome talons.

We must go elsewhere
Than the cry of the hoot owl,
Somewhere beyond realism,
For the tone of the poetical.

RICHARD EBERHART

To an Old Lady

Ripeness is all; her in her cooling planet
Revere; do not presume to think her wasted.
Project her no projectile, plan nor man it;
Gods cool in turn, by the sun long outlasted.

Our earth alone given no name of god
Gives, too, no hold for such a leap to aid her;
Landing, you break some palace and seem odd;
Bees sting their need, the keeper's queen invader.

No, to your telescope; spy out the land;
Watch while her ritual is still to see,
Still stand her temples emptying in the sand
Whose waves o'erthrew their crumbled tracery;

Still stand uncalled-on her soul's appanage;
Much social detail whose successor fades,
Wit used to run a house and to play Bridge,
And tragic fervour, to dismiss her maids.

Years her precession do not throw from gear.
She reads a compass certain of her pole;
Confident, finds no confines on her sphere,
Whose failing crops are in her sole control.

Stars how much further from me fill my night,
Strange that she too should be inaccessible,
Who shares my sun. He curtains her from sight,
And but in darkness is she visible.

WILLIAM EMPSON

Ikey on the People of Hellya

Rognvald who stalks round Corse with his stick
I do not love.
His dog has a loud sharp mouth.
The wood of his door is very hard.
Once, tangled in his barbed wire
(I was paying respect to his hens, stroking a wing)
He laid his stick on me.
That was out of a hard forest also.

Mansie at Quoy is a biddable man.
Ask for water, he gives you rum.
I strip his scarecrow April by April,
Ask for a scattering of straw in his byre
He lays you down
Under a quilt as long and light as heaven.
Then only his raging woman spoils our peace.

Gray the fisherman is no trouble now
Who quoted me the vagrancy laws
In a voice slippery as seaweed under the kirkyard.
I rigged his boat with the seven curses.
Occasionally still, for encouragement,
I put the knife in his net.

Though she has black peats and a yellow hill
And fifty silken cattle
I do not go near Merran and her cats.
Rather break a crust on a tombstone.
Her great-great-grandmother
Wore the red coat at Gallowsha.

The thousand rabbits of Hollandsay
Keep Simpson's corn short,
Whereby comes much cruelty, gas and gunshot.
Tonight I have lit a small fire.
I have stained my knife red.
I have peeled a round turnip.
And I pray the Lord
To preserve those nine hundred and ninety nine innocents.

Finally in Folscroft lives Jeems,
Tailor and undertaker, a crosser of limbs,
One tape for the living and the dead.
He brings a needle to my rags in winter,
And he guards, against my stillness,
The seven white boards
I got from the Danish wreck one winter.

GEORGE MACKAY BROWN

112

Parliament Hill Fields

Rumbling under blackened girders, Midland, bound for
    Cricklewood,
Puffed its sulphur to the sunset where that Land of Laundries
    stood,
Rumble under, thunder over, train and tram alternate go,
Shake the floor and smudge the ledger, Charrington, Sells,
    Dale and Co.,
Nuts and nuggets in the window, trucks along the lines below.

When the Bon Marché was shuttered, when the feet were
    hot and tired,
Outside Charrington's we waited, by the "STOP HERE IF
    REQUIRED",
Launched aboard the shopping basket, sat precipitately down,
Rocked past Zwanziger the baker's, and the terrace blackish
    brown,
And the curious Anglo-Norman parish church of Kentish
    Town.

Till the tram went over thirty, sighting terminus again,
Past municipal lawn tennis and the bobble-hanging plane;
Soft the light suburban evening caught our ashlar-speckled
    spire,
Eighteen-sixty Early English, as the mighty elms retire
Either side of Brookfield Mansions flashing fine French-
    window fire.

Oh the after-tram-ride quiet, when we heard a mile beyond,
Silver music from the bandstand, barking dogs by Highgate
    Pond;
Up the hill where stucco houses in Virginia creeper drown—
And my childish wave of pity, seeing children carrying down
Sheaves of drooping dandelions to the courts of Kentish Town.

JOHN BETJEMAN

The Unknown

She is most fair,
And when they see her pass
The poets' ladies
Look no more in the glass
But after her.

On a bleak moor
Running under the moon
She lures a poet,
Once proud or happy, soon
Far from his door.

Beside a train,
Because they saw her go,
Or failed to see her,
Travellers and watchers know
Another pain.

The simple lack
Of her is more to me
Than others' presence,
Whether life splendid be
Or utter black.

I have not seen,
I have no news of her;
I can tell only
She is not here, but there
She might have been.

She is to be kissed
Only perhaps by me;
She may be seeking
Me and no other; she
May not exist.

EDWARD THOMAS

The Shield of Achilles

She looked over his shoulder
        For vines and olive trees,
Marble well-governed cities
        And ships upon untamed seas,
But there on the shining metal
        His hands had put instead
An artificial wilderness
        And a sky like lead.

A plain without a feature, bare and brown,
    No blade of grass, no sign of neighbourhood,
Nothing to eat and nowhere to sit down,
    Yet, congregated on its blankness, stood
    An unintelligible multitude,
A million eyes, a million boots in line,
Without expression, waiting for a sign.

Out of the air a voice without a face
    Proved by statistics that some cause was just
In tones as dry and level as the place:
    No one was cheered and nothing was discussed;
    Column by column in a cloud of dust
They marched away enduring a belief
Whose logic brought them, somewhere else, to grief.

She looked over his shoulder
        For ritual pieties,
White flower-garlanded heifers,
        Libation and sacrifice,
But there on the shining metal
        Where the altar should have been,
She saw by his flickering forge-light
        Quite another scene.

Barbed wire enclosed an arbitrary spot
　　Where bored officials lounged (one cracked a joke)
And sentries sweated for the day was hot:
　　A crowd of ordinary decent folk
　　Watched from without and neither moved nor spoke
As three pale figures were led forth and bound
To three posts driven upright in the ground.

The mass and majesty of this world, all
　　That carries weight and always weighs the same
Lay in the hands of others; they were small
　　And could not hope for help and no help came:
　　What their foes liked to do was done, their shame
Was all the worst could wish; they lost their pride
And died as men before their bodies died.

　　　　She looked over his shoulder
　　　　　　For athletes at their games,
　　　　Men and women in a dance
　　　　　　Moving their sweet limbs
　　　　Quick, quick, to music,
　　　　　　But there on the shining shield
　　　　His hands had set no dancing-floor
　　　　　　But a weed-choked field.

A ragged urchin, aimless and alone,
　　Loitered about that vacancy, a bird
Flew up to safety from his well-aimed stone:
　　That girls are raped, that two boys knife a third,
　　Were axioms to him, who'd never heard
Of any world where promises were kept,
Or one could weep because another wept.

The thin-lipped armourer,
  Hephaestos hobbled away,
Thetis of the shining breasts
  Cried out in dismay
At what the god had wrought
  To please her son, the strong
Iron-hearted man-slaying Achilles
  Who would not live long.

W. H. AUDEN

Birmingham

Smoke from the train-gulf hid by hoardings blunders upward,
    the brakes of cars
Pipe as the policeman pivoting round raises his flat hand, bars
With his figure of a monolith Pharaoh the queue of fidgety
    machines
(Chromium dogs on the bonnet, faces behind the triplex
    screens).
Behind him the streets run away between the proud glass of
    shops,
Cubical scent-bottles artificial legs arctic foxes and electric
    mops,
But beyond this centre the slumward vista thins like a diagram:
There, unvisited, are Vulcan's forges who doesn't care a
    tinker's damn.

Splayed outwards through the suburbs houses, houses for rest
Seducingly rigged by the builder, half-timbered houses with
    lips pressed
So tightly and eyes staring at the traffic through bleary haws
And only a six-inch grip of the racing earth in their concrete
    claws;
In these houses men as in a dream pursue the Platonic Forms
With wireless and cairn terriers and gadgets approximating to
    the fickle norms
And endeavour to find God and score one over the neighbour
By climbing tentatively upward on jerry-built beauty and
    sweated labour.

The lunch hour: the shops empty, shopgirls' faces relax
Diaphanous as green glass, empty as old almanacs
As incoherent with ticketed gewgaws tiered behind their heads
As the Burne-Jones windows in St. Philip's broken by
    crawling leads;
Insipid colour, patches of emotion, Saturday thrills

(This theatre is sprayed with "June")—the gutter take our
   old playbills,
Next week-end it is likely in the heart's funfair we shall pull
Strong enough on the handle to get back our money; or at any
   rate it is possible.

On shining lines the trams like vast sarcophagi move
Into the sky, plum after sunset, merging to duck's egg, barred
   with mauve
Zeppelin clouds, and Pentecost-like the cars' headlights bud
Out from sideroads and the traffic signals, crême-de-menthe or
   bull's blood,
Tell one to stop, the engine gently breathing, or to go on
To where like black pipes of organs in the frayed and fading
   zone
Of the West the factory chimneys on sullen sentry will all
   night wait
To call, in the harsh morning, sleep-stupid faces through the
   daily gate.

                                        LOUIS MACNEICE

La Figlia che Piange

O quam te memorem virgo . . .

Stand on the highest pavement of the stair—
Lean on a garden urn—
Weave, weave the sunlight in your hair—
Clasp your flowers to you with a pained surprise—
Fling them to the ground and turn
With a fugitive resentment in your eyes:
But weave, weave the sunlight in your hair.

So I would have had him leave,
So I would have had her stand and grieve,
So he would have left
As the soul leaves the body torn and bruised,
As the mind deserts the body it has used.
I should find
Some way incomparably light and deft,
Some way we both should understand,
Simple and faithless as a smile and shake of the hand.

She turned away, but with the autumn weather
Compelled my imagination many days,
Many days and many hours:
Her hair over her arms and her arms full of flowers.
And I wonder how they should have been together!
I should have lost a gesture and a pose.
Sometimes these cogitations still amaze
The troubled midnight and the noon's repose.

                                                T. S. ELIOT

Sailing to Byzantium

I

That is no country for old men. The young
In one another's arms, birds in the trees
—Those dying generations—at their song,
The salmon-falls, the mackerel-crowded seas,
Fish, flesh, or fowl, commend all summer long
Whatever is begotten, born, and dies.
Caught in that sensual music all neglect
Monuments of unageing intellect.

II

An aged man is but a paltry thing,
A tattered coat upon a stick, unless
Soul clap its hands and sing, and louder sing
For every tatter in its mortal dress,
Nor is there singing school but studying
Monuments of its own magnificence;
And therefore I have sailed the seas and come
To the holy city of Byzantium.

III

O sages standing in God's holy fire
As in the gold mosaic of a wall,
Come from the holy fire, perne in a gyre,
And be the singing-masters of my soul.
Consume my heart away; sick with desire
And fastened to a dying animal
It knows not what it is; and gather me
Into the artifice of eternity.

Once out of nature I shall never take
My bodily form from any natural thing,
But such a form as Grecian goldsmiths make
Of hammered gold and gold enamelling
To keep a drowsy Emperor awake;
Or set upon a golden bough to sing
To lords and ladies of Byzantium
Of what is past, or passing, or to come.

W. B. YEATS

The Bull of Bendylaw

The black bull bellowed before the sea.
The sea, till that day orderly,
Hove up against Bendylaw.

The queen in the mulberry arbour stared
Stiff as a queen on a playing card.
The king fingered his beard.

A blue sea, four horny bull-feet,
A bull-snouted sea that wouldn't stay put,
Bucked at the garden gate.

Along box-lined walks in the florid sun
Toward the rowdy bellow and back again
The lords and ladies ran.

The great bronze gate began to crack,
The sea broke in at every crack,
Pellmell, blueblack.

The bull surged up, the bull surged down,
Not to be stayed by a daisy chain
Nor by any learned man.

O the king's tidy acre is under the sea,
And the royal rose in the bull's belly,
And the bull on the king's highway.

SYLVIA PLATH

On the Move

"Man, you gotta Go"

The blue jay scuffling in the bushes follows
Some hidden purpose, and the gust of birds
That spurts across the field, the wheeling swallows,
Have nested in the trees and undergrowth.
Seeking their instinct, or their poise, or both,
One moves with an uncertain violence
Under the dust thrown by a baffled sense
Or the dull thunder of approximate words.

On motorcycles, up the road, they come:
Small, black, as flies hanging in heat, the Boys,
Until the distance throws them forth, their hum
Bulges to thunder held by calf and thigh.
In goggles, donned impersonality,
In gleaming jackets trophied with the dust,
They strap in doubt—by hiding it, robust—
And almost hear a meaning in their noise.

Exact conclusion of their hardiness
Has no shape yet, but from known whereabouts
They ride, direction where the tires press.
They scare a flight of birds across the field:
Much that is natural, to the will must yield.
Men manufacture both machine and soul,
And use what they imperfectly control
To dare a future from the taken routes.

It is a part solution, after all.
One is not necessarily discord
On earth; or damned because, half animal,
One lacks direct instinct, because one wakes
Afloat on movement that divides and breaks.
One joins the movement in a valueless world,
Choosing it, till, both hurler and the hurled,
One moves as well, always toward, toward.

A minute holds them, who have come to go:
The self-defined, astride the created will
They burst away; the towns they travel through
Are home for neither bird nor holiness,
For birds and saints complete their purposes.
At worst, one is in motion; and at best,
Reaching no absolute, in which to rest,
One is always nearer by not keeping still.

California

THOM GUNN

The Flower-fed Buffaloes

The flower-fed buffaloes of the spring
In the days of long ago,
Ranged where the locomotives sing
And the prairie flowers lie low:—
The tossing, blooming, perfumed grass
Is swept away by the wheat,
Wheels and wheels and wheels spin by
In the spring that still is sweet.
But the flower-fed buffaloes of the spring
Left us, long ago.
They gore no more, they bellow no more,
They trundle around the hills no more:—
With the Blackfeet, lying low,
With the Pawnees, lying low,
Lying low.

VACHEL LINDSAY

Ultima Ratio Regum

The guns spell money's ultimate reason
In letters of lead on the Spring hillside.
But the boy lying dead under the olive trees
Was too young and too silly
To have been notable to their important eye.
He was a better target for a kiss.

When he lived, tall factory hooters never summoned him
Nor did restaurant plate-glass doors revolve to wave him in
His name never appeared in the papers.
The world maintained its traditional wall
Round the dead with their gold sunk deep as a well,
While his life, intangible as a Stock Exchange rumour,
   drifted outside.

O too lightly he threw down his cap
One day when the breeze threw petals from the trees.
The unflowering wall sprouted with guns,
Machine-gun anger quickly scythed the grasses;
Flags and leaves fell from hands and branches;
The tweed cap rotted in the nettles.

Consider his life which was valueless
In terms of employment, hotel ledgers, news files.
Consider. One bullet in ten thousand kills a man.
Ask. Was so much expenditure justified
On the death of one so young, and so silly
Lying under the olive trees, O world, O death?

STEPHEN SPENDER

The Images of Death

The hawk, the furred eagle, the smooth panther—
Images of desire and power, images of death,
These we adore and fear, these we need,
Move in the solitude of night or the tall sky,
Move with a strict grace to the one fulfilment:
The Greenland falcon, the beautiful one,
Lives on carrion and dives inevitably to the prey.

To be human is more difficult:
To be human is to know oneself, to hold the broken mirror,
To become aware of justice, truth, mercy,
To choose the difficult road, to aim
Crookedly, for the direct aim is failure,
To abandon the way of the hawk and the grey falcon.

These fall, and fall stupidly:
To be human is to fall, but not stupidly;
To suffer, but not for a simple end;
To choose, and know the penalty of choice;
To read the intensity of human eyes and features;
To know the intricacy of life and the value of death;
To remember the furred eagle and the smooth panther,
The images of death, and death's simplicity.

MICHAEL ROBERTS

The Choice

The intellect of man is forced to choose
Perfection of the life, or of the work,
And if it take the second must refuse
A heavenly mansion, raging in the dark.

When all that story's finished, what's the news?
In luck or out the toil has left its mark:
That old perplexity an empty purse,
Or the day's vanity, the night's remorse.

W. B. YEATS

The Ivy and the Ash

The ivy and the ash
cast a dark arm
across the beck.
In this rocky ghyll
I sit and watch
the eye-iris water move
like muscles over stones
smooth'd by this ageless action.

The water brings
from the high fell
an icy current of air.
There is no sun to splinter
the grey visionary quartz.
The heart is cool
and adamant among the rocks
mottled with wet moss.

Descend into the valley
explore the plain
even the salt sea
but keep the heart
cool in the memory
of ivy, ash
and the glistening beck
running swiftly through the black rocks.

HERBERT READ

A Glass of Beer

The lanky hank of a she in the inn over there
Nearly killed me for asking the loan of a glass of beer;
May the devil grip the whey-faced slut by the hair,
And beat bad manners out of her skin for a year.

That parboiled ape, with the toughest jaw you will see
On virtue's path, and a voice that would rasp the dead,
Came roaring and raging the minute she looked at me,
And threw me out of the house on the back of my head!

If I asked her master he'd give me a cask a day;
But she, with the beer at hand, not a gill would arrange!
May she marry a ghost and bear him a kitten, and may
The High King of Glory permit her to get the mange.

JAMES STEPHENS

Dead Boy

The little cousin is dead, by foul subtraction,
A green bough from Virginia's aged tree,
And none of the county kin like the transaction,
Nor some of the world of outer dark, like me.

A boy not beautiful, nor good, nor clever,
A black cloud full of storms too hot for keeping,
A sword beneath his mother's heart—yet never
Woman bewept her babe as this is weeping.

A pig with a pasty face, so I had said,
Squealing for cookies, kinned by poor pretence
With a noble house. But the little man quite dead,
I see the forebears' antique lineaments.

The elder men have strode by the box of death
To the wide flag porch, and muttering low send round
The bruit of the day. O friendly waste of breath!
Their hearts are hurt with a deep dynastic wound.

He was pale and little, the foolish neighbors say;
The first-fruits, saith the Preacher, the Lord hath taken;
But this was the old tree's late branch wrenched away,
Grieving the sapless limbs, the shorn and shaken.

JOHN CROWE RANSOM

Fortune

The natural silence of a tree
The motion of a mast upon the fresh-tossing sea
Now foam-inclined, now to the sun with dignity

Or the stone brow of a mountain
Regarded from a town, or the curvet fountain
Or one street-stopped in wonder at the fountain

Or a great cloud entering the room of the sky
Napoleon of his century
Heard come to knowing music consciously

Such, not us, reflect and have their day
We are but vapour of today
Unless love's chance fall on us and call us away

As the wind takes what it can
And blowing on the fortunate face, reveals the man.

CHARLES MADGE

Aristocrats

"I think I am becoming a God"

The noble horse with courage in his eye
clean in the bone, looks up at a shellburst:
away fly the images of the shires
but he puts the pipe back in his mouth.

Peter was unfortunately killed by an 88:
it took his leg away, he died in the ambulance.
I saw him crawling on the sand; he said
It's most unfair, they've shot my foot off.

How can I live among this gentle
obsolescent breed of heroes, and not weep?
Unicorns, almost,
for they are falling into two legends
in which their stupidity and chivalry
are celebrated. Each, fool and hero, will be an
    immortal.

The plains were their cricket pitch
and in the mountains the tremendous drop fences
brought down some of the runners. Here then
under the stones and earth they dispose themselves,
I think with their famous unconcern.
It is not gunfire I hear but a hunting horn.

Enfidaville, Tunisia, 1943

KEITH DOUGLAS

Snow

The room was suddenly rich and the great bay-window was
Spawning snow and pink roses against it
Soundlessly collateral and incompatible:
World is suddener than we fancy it.

World is crazier and more of it than we think,
Incorrigibly plural. I peel and portion
A tangerine and spit the pips and feel
The drunkenness of things being various.

And the fire flames with a bubbling sound for world
Is more spiteful and gay than one supposes—
On the tongue on the eyes on the ears in the palms of one's
    hands—
There is more than glass between the snow and the huge roses.

LOUIS MACNEICE

Spring Voices

The small householder now comes out warily
Afraid of the barrage of sun that shouts cheerily,
Spring is massing forces, birds wink in air,
The battlemented chestnuts volley green fire,
The pigeons banking on the wind, the hoots of cars,
Stir him to run wild, gamble on horses, buy cigars;
Joy lies before him to be ladled and lapped from his hand—
Only that behind him, in the shade of his villa, memories
    stand
Breathing on his neck and muttering that all this has happened
    before,
Keep the wind out, cast no clout, try no unwarranted jaunts
    untried before,
But let the spring slide by nor think to board its car
For it rides West to where the tangles of scrap-iron are;
Do not walk, these voices say, between the bucking clouds
    alone
Or you may loiter into a suddenly howling crater, or fall,
    jerked back, garrotted by the sun.

LOUIS MACNEICE

Spate in Winter Midnight

The streams fall down and through the darkness bear
Such wild and shaking hair,
Such looks beyond a cool surmise,
Such lamentable uproar from night skies
As turn the owl from honey of blood and make
Great stags stand still to hear the darkness shake.

Through Troys of bracken and Babel towers of rocks
Shrinks now the looting fox,
Fearful to touch the thudding ground
And flattened to it by the mastering sound.
And roebuck stilt and leap sideways; their skin
Twitches like water on the fear within.

Black hills are slashed white with this falling grace
Whose violence buckles space
To a sheet-iron thunder. This
Is noise made universe, whose still centre is
Where the cold adder sleeps in his small bed,
Curled neatly round his neat and evil head.

NORMAN MacCAIG

Preludes

I

The winter evening settles down
With smell of steaks in passageways.
Six o'clock.
The burnt-out ends of smoky days.
And now a gusty shower wraps
The grimy scraps
Of withered leaves about your feet
And newspapers from vacant lots;
The showers beat
On broken blinds and chimney-pots,
And at the corner of the street
A lonely cab-horse steams and stamps.
And then the lighting of the lamps.

II

The morning comes to consciousness
Of faint stale smells of beer
From the sawdust-trampled street
With all its muddy feet that press
To early coffee-stands.
With the other masquerades
That time resumes,
One thinks of all the hands
That are raising dingy shades
In a thousand furnished rooms.

III

You tossed a blanket from the bed,
You lay upon your back, and waited;
You dozed, and watched the night revealing
The thousand sordid images

Of which your soul was constituted;
They flickered against the ceiling.
And when all the world came back
And the light crept up between the shutters
And you heard the sparrows in the gutters,
You had such a vision of the street
As the street hardly understands;
Sitting along the bed's edge, where
You curled the papers from your hair,
Or clasped the yellow soles of feet
In the palms of both soiled hands.

IV

His soul stretched tight across the skies
That fade behind a city block,
Or trampled by insistent feet
At four and five and six o'clock;
And short square fingers stuffing pipes,
And evening newspapers, and eyes
Assured of certain certainties,
The conscience of a blackened street
Impatient to assume the world.

I am moved by fancies that are curled
Around these images, and cling:
The notion of some infinitely gentle
Infinitely suffering thing.

Wipe your hand across your mouth, and laugh;
The worlds revolve like ancient women
Gathering fuel in vacant lots.

T. S. ELIOT

Carol

There was a Boy bedded in bracken,
Like to a sleeping snake all curled he lay,
On his thin navel turned this spinning sphere,
Each feeble finger fetched seven suns away,
He was not dropped in good-for-lambing weather,
He took no suck when shook buds sing together,
But he is come in cold-as-workhouse weather,
    Poor as a Salford child.

JOHN SHORT

The Gallows

There was a weasel lived in the sun
With all his family,
Till a keeper shot him with his gun
And hung him up on a tree,
Where he swings in the wind and rain,
In the sun and in the snow,
Without pleasure, without pain,
On the dead oak tree bough.

There was a crow who was no sleeper,
But a thief and a murderer
Till a very late hour; and this keeper
Made him one of the things that were,
To hang and flap in rain and wind,
In the sun and in the snow.
There are no more sins to be sinned
On the dead oak tree bough.

There was a magpie, too,
Had a long tongue and a long tail.
He could both talk and do—
But what did that avail?
He, too, flaps in the wind and rain
Alongside weasel and crow,
Without pleasure, without pain,
On the dead oak tree bough.

And many other beasts
And birds, skin, bone, and feather,
Have been taken from their feasts
And hung up there together,
To swing and have endless leisure
In the sun and in the snow,
Without pain, without pleasure,
On the dead oak tree bough.

EDWARD THOMAS

Black Rock of Kiltearn

They named it Aultgraat—Ugly Burn,
This water through the crevice hurled
Scouring the entrails of the world—
Not ugly in the rising smoke
That clothes it with a rainbowed cloak.
But slip a foot on frost-spiked stone
Above this rock-lipped Phlegethon
And you shall have
The Black Rock of Kiltearn
For tombstone, grave
And trumpet of your resurrection.

ANDREW YOUNG

Grandparents

They're altogether otherworldly now,
those adults champing for their ritual Friday spin
to pharmacist and five-and-ten in Brockton.
Back in my throw-away and shaggy span
of adolescence, Grandpa still waves his stick
like a policeman;
Grandmother, like a Mohammedan, still wears her thick
lavender mourning and touring veil,
the Pierce Arrow clears its throat in a horse-stall.
Then the dry road dust rises to whiten
the fatigued elm leaves—
the nineteenth century, tired of children, is gone.
They're all gone into a world of light; the farm's my own.

The farm's my own!
Back there alone,
I keep indoors, and spoil another season.
I hear the rattley little country gramophone
racking its five foot horn:
"O Summer Time!"
Even at noon here the formidable
Ancien Régime still keeps nature at a distance. Five
green shaded light bulbs spider the billiards-table,
no field is greener than its cloth,
where Grandpa, dipping sugar for us both,
once spilled his demitasse.
His favourite ball, the number three,
still hides the coffee stain.

Never again
to walk there, chalk our cues,
insist on shooting for us both.
Grandpa! Have me, hold me, cherish me!
Tears smut my fingers. There
half my life-lease later,
I hold an *Illustrated London News*,
disloyal still,
I doodle handlebar
mustaches on the last Russian Czar.

ROBERT LOWELL

The Caves

This is the cave of which I spoke,
These are the blackened stones, and these
Our footprints, seven lives ago.

Darkness was in the cave like shifting smoke,
Stalagmites grew like equatorial trees,
There was a pool, quite black and silent, seven lives ago.

Here such a one turned back, and there
Another stumbled and his nerve gave out;
Men have escaped blindly, they know not how.

Our candles gutter in the mouldering air,
Here the rock fell, beyond a doubt,
There was no light in those days, and there is none now.

Water drips from the roof, and the caves narrow,
Galleries lead downward to the unknown dark;
This was the point we reached, the farthest known.

Here someone in the debris found an arrow,
Men have been here before, and left their mark
Scratched on the limestone wall with splintered bone.

Here the dark word was said for memory's sake,
And lost, here on the cold sand, to the puzzled brow:

This was the farthest point, the fabled lake:
These were our footprints, seven lives ago.

MICHAEL ROBERTS

Horses

Those lumbering horses in the steady plough,
On the bare field—I wonder why, just now,
They seemed terrible, so wild and strange,
Like magic power on the stony grange.

Perhaps some childish hour has come again,
When I watched fearful, through the blackening rain,
Their hooves like pistons in an ancient mill
Move up and down, yet seem as standing still.

Their conquering hooves which trod the stubble down
Were ritual that turned the field to brown,
And their great hulks were seraphim of gold,
Or mute ecstatic monsters on the mould.

And oh the rapture, when, one furrow done,
They marched broad-breasted to the sinking sun!
The light flowed off their bossy sides in flakes;
The furrows rolled behind like struggling snakes.

But when at dusk with steaming nostrils home
They came, they seemed gigantic in the gloam,
And warm and glowing with mysterious fire
That lit their smouldering bodies in the mire.

Their eyes as brilliant and as wide as night
Gleamed with a cruel apocalyptic light.
Their manes the leaping ire of the wind
Lifted with rage invisible and blind.

Ah, now it fades! it fades! and I must pine
Again for that dread country crystalline,
Where the blank field and the still-standing tree
Were bright and fearful presences to me.

EDWIN MUIR

Vergissmeinicht

Three weeks gone and the combatants gone,
returning over the nightmare ground
we found the place again, and found
the soldier sprawling in the sun.

The frowning barrel of his gun
overshadowing. As we came on
that day, he hit my tank with one
like the entry of a demon.

Look. Here in the gunpit spoil
the dishonoured picture of his girl
who has put: *Steffi. Vergissmeinicht*
in a copybook gothic script.

We see him almost with content
abased, and seeming to have paid
and mocked at by his own equipment
that's hard and good when he's decayed.

But she would weep to see today
how on his skin the swart flies move;
the dust upon the paper eye
and the burst stomach like a cave.

For here the lover and killer are mingled
who had one body and one heart.
And death who had the soldier singled
has done the lover mortal hurt.

Homs, Tripolitania, 1943

KEITH DOUGLAS

The Arctic Ox (or Goat)

Derived from "Golden Fleece of the Arctic",
by John J. Teal, Jr., who rears musk oxen on
his farm in Vermont, as set forth by him in
the March 1958 issue of the *Atlantic Monthly*.

To wear the arctic fox
You have to kill it. Wear
   qiviut—the underwool of the arctic ox—
pulled off it like a sweater;
your coat is warm; your conscience better.

I would like a suit of
qiviut, so light I did not
   know I had it on; and in the
course of time, another
since I had not had to murder

the "goat" that grew the fleece
that made the first. The musk ox
   has no musk and it is not an ox—
illiterate epithet.
Bury your nose in one when wet.

It smells of water, nothing else,
and browses goatlike on
   hind legs. Its great distinction
is not egocentric scent
but that it is intelligent.

Chinchillas, otters, water-rats,
and beavers, keep us warm
   but think! a "musk ox" grows six pounds
of *qiviut*; the cashmere ram,
three ounces—that is all—of pashm.

Lying in an exposed spot,
basking in the blizzard,
   these ponderosos could dominate
the rare-hairs market in Kashan and yet
you could not have a choicer pet.

They join you as you work;
love jumping in and out of holes,
   play in water with the children,
learn fast, know their names,
will open gates and invent games.

While not incapable
of courtship, they may find its
   servitude and flutter, too much
like Procrustes' bed;
so some decide to stay unwed.

Camels are snobbish
and sheep, unintelligent;
   water buffaloes, neurasthenic—
even murderous.
Reindeer seem over-serious.

Whereas these scarce *qivies*,
with golden fleece and winning ways,
   outstripping every fur-bearer—
there in Vermont quiet—
could demand Bold Ruler's diet:

Mountain Valley water,
dandelions, carrots, oats—
   encouraged as well by bed
made fresh three times a day—
to roll and revel in the hay.

Insatiable for willow
leaves alone, our goatlike
   qivi-curvi-capricornus
sheds down ideal for a nest.
Song-birds find *qiviut* best.

Suppose you had a bag
of it; you could spin a pound
   into a twenty-four-or-five-
mile thread—one, forty-ply—
that will not shrink in any dye.

If you fear that you are
reading an advertisement,
   you are. If we can't be cordial
to these creatures' fleece,
I think that we deserve to freeze.

MARIANNE MOORE

Coole Park and Ballylee, 1931

Under my window-ledge the waters race,
Otters below and moor-hens on the top,
Run for a mile undimmed in Heaven's face
Then darkening through "dark" Raftery's "cellar" drop,
Run underground, rise in a rocky place
In Coole demesne, and there to finish up
Spread to a lake and drop into a hole.
What's water but the generated soul?

Upon the border of that lake's a wood
Now all dry sticks under a wintry sun,
And in a copse of beeches there I stood,
For Nature's pulled her tragic buskin on
And all the rant's a mirror of my mood:
At sudden thunder of the mounting swan
I turned about and looked where branches break
The glittering reaches of the flooded lake.

Another emblem there! That stormy white
But seems a concentration of the sky;
And, like the soul, it sails into the sight
And in the morning's gone, no man knows why;
And is so lovely that it sets to right
What knowledge or its lack had set awry,
So arrogantly pure, a child might think
It can be murdered with a spot of ink.

Sound of a stick upon the floor, a sound
From somebody that toils from chair to chair;
Beloved books that famous hands have bound,
Old marble heads, old pictures everywhere;
Great rooms where travelled men and children found
Content or joy; a last inheritor
Where none has reigned that lacked a name and fame
Or out of folly into folly came.

A spot whereon the founders lived and died
Seemed once more dear than life; ancestral trees,
Or gardens rich in memory glorified
Marriages, alliances and families,
And every bride's ambition satisfied.
Where fashion or mere fantasy decrees
We shift about—all that great glory spent—
Like some poor Arab tribesman and his tent.

We were the last romantics—chose for theme
Traditional sanctity and loveliness;
Whatever's written in what poets name
The book of the people; whatever most can bless
The mind of man or elevate a rhyme;
But all is changed, that high horse riderless,
Though mounted in that saddle Homer rode
Where the swans drift upon a darkening flood.

W. B. YEATS

Man about to Enter Sea

Walking into the summer cold sea
arms folded
trying to keep the wave and frolicy bather
splashings from further chilling him
He moves as if not to—but I know
he'll eventually go with a NOW IN! and
become warm—

That curious warm is all too familiar
as when frogs from fish kicked
and fins winged flew
and whatever it was decided lungs
and a chance in the change above the sea—

There he wades millions of years that are legs
back into that biggest and strangest of wombs
He stands—the sea is up to his belly button
—He would it nothing more than a holiday's dip

But I feel he's algae for skin
He who calls the dinosaur his unfortunate brother
And what with crawling anthropods
oh they're only bathers on a summer shore
yet it is possible to drown in a surface of air
deem the entire earth one NOW IN! and once in
fated out again—

GREGORY CORSO

Suburban Dream

Walking the suburbs in the afternoon
In summer when the idle doors stand open
   And the air flows through the rooms
   Fanning the curtain hems,

You wander through a cool elysium
Of women, schoolgirls, children, garden talks,
   With a schoolboy here and there
   Conning his history book.

The men are all away in offices,
Committee-rooms, laboratories, banks,
   Or pushing cotton goods
   In Wick or Ilfracombe.

The massed unanimous absence liberates
The light keys of the piano and sets free
   Chopin and everlasting youth,
   Now, with the masters gone.

And all things turn to images of peace,
The boy curled over his book, the young girl poised
   On the path as if beguiled
   By the silence of a wood.

It is a child's dream of a grown-up world
But soon the brazen evening clocks will bring
   The tramp of feet and brisk
   Fanfare of motor horns
   And the masters come.

EDWIN MUIR

By Ferry to the Island

We crossed by ferry to the bare island
where sheep and cows stared coldly through the wind—
the sea behind us with its silver water,
the silent ferryman standing in the stern
clutching his coat about him like old iron.

We landed from the ferry and went inland
past a small church down to the winding shore
where a white seagull fallen from the failing
chill and ancient daylight lay so pure
and softly breasted that it made more dear

the lesser white around us. There we sat
sheltered by a rock beside the sea.
Someone made coffee, someone played the fool
in a high rising voice for two hours.
The sea's language was more grave and harsh.

And one sat there whose dress was white and cool.
The fool sparkled his wit that she might hear
new diamonds turning on her naked finger.
What might the sea think or the dull sheep
lifting its head through heavy Sunday sleep?

And later, going home, a moon rising
at the end of a cart-track, minimum of red,
the wind being dark, imperfect cows staring
out of their half-intelligence, and a plough
lying on its side in the cold, raw

naked twilight, there began to move
slowly, like heavy water, in the heart
the image of the gull and of that dress,
both being white and out of the darkness rising
the moon ahead of us with its rusty ring.

IAIN CRICHTON-SMITH

"Blackie, the Electric Rembrandt"

We watch through the shop-front while
Blackie draws stars—an equal

concentration on his and
the youngster's faces. The hand

is steady and accurate;
but the boy does not see it

for his eyes follow the point
that touches (quick, dark movement!)

a virginal arm beneath
his rolled sleeve: he holds his breath.

. . . Now that it is finished, he
hands a few bills to Blackie

and leaves with a bandage on
his arm, under which gleam ten

stars, hanging in a blue thick
cluster. Now he is starlike.

THOM GUNN

A Dream of Horses

We were born grooms, in stable-straw we sleep still,
All our wealth horse-dung and the combings of horses,
And all we can talk about is what horses ail.

Out of the night that gulfed beyond the palace-gate
There shook hooves and hooves and hooves of horses:
Our horses battered their stalls; their eyes jerked white.

And we ran out, mice in our pockets and straw in our hair,
Into darkness that was avalanching to horses
And a quake of hooves. Our lantern's little orange flare

Made a round mask of our each sleep-dazed face,
Bodiless, or else bodied by horses
That whinnied and bit and cannoned the world from its place.

The tall palace was so white, the moon was so round,
Everything else this plunging of horses
To the rim of our eyes that strove for the shapes of the sound.

We crouched at our lantern, our bodies drank the din,
And we longed for a death trampled by such horses
As every grain of the earth had hooves and mane.

We must have fallen like drunkards into a dream
Of listening, lulled by the thunder of the horses.
We awoke stiff; broad day had come.

Out through the gate the unprinted desert stretched
To stone and scorpion; our stable-horses
Lay in their straw, in a hag-sweat, listless and wretched.

Now let us, tied, be quartered by these poor horses,
If but doomsday's flames be great horses,
The forever itself a circling of the hooves of horses.

TED HUGHES

154

Marina

Quis hic locus, quae
regio, quae mundi plaga?

What seas what shores what grey rocks and what islands
What water lapping the bow
And scent of pine and the woodthrush singing through the fog
What images return
O my daughter.

Those who sharpen the tooth of the dog, meaning
Death
Those who glitter with the glory of the hummingbird, meaning
Death
Those who sit in the stye of contentment, meaning
Death
Those who suffer the ecstasy of the animals, meaning
Death

Are become unsubstantial, reduced by a wind,
A breath of pine, and the woodsong fog
By this grace dissolved in place

What is this face, less clear and clearer
The pulse in the arm, less strong and stronger—
Given or lent? more distant than stars and nearer than the eye

Whispers and small laughter between leaves and hurrying feet
Under sleep, where all the waters meet.

Bowsprit cracked with ice and paint cracked with heat.
I made this, I have forgotten
And remember.
The rigging weak and the canvas rotten
Between one June and another September.
Made this unknowing, half conscious, unknown, my own.

The garboard strake leaks, the seams need caulking.
This form, this face, this life
Living to live in a world of time beyond me; let me
Resign my life for this life, my speech for that unspoken,
The awakened, lips parted, the hope, the new ships.

What seas what shores what granite islands towards my timbers
And woodthrush calling through the fog
My daughter.

T. S. ELIOT

Spoils

When all is over and you march for home,
The spoils of war are easily disposed of:
Standards, weapons of combat, helmets, drums
May decorate a staircase or a study,
While lesser gleanings of the battlefield—
Coins, watches, wedding-rings, gold teeth and such—
Are sold anonymously for solid cash.

The spoils of love present a different case,
When all is over and you march for home:
That lock of hair, these letters and the portrait
May not be publicly displayed; nor sold;
Nor burned; nor returned (the heart being obstinate)—
Yet never dare entrust them to a safe
For fear they burn a hole through two-foot steel.

ROBERT GRAVES

The Hero

When the hero's task was done,
And the beast lay underground,
In the time that he had won
From the fates that pushed him round

He had time to contemplate
How the peasants still were bled
And that in the salvaged state
Worms continued at the head.

Little space: already, where
Sweetly he enjoyed his fish,
Seeing through the shouldered hair
Loosening sails and dirty dish,

Gasped a pale new plea for aid.
Cleaning his gun later, he
Felt with awe the old beast's shade
Fall across the wine-dark sea.

ROY FULLER

The River-Merchant's Wife: a Letter

While my hair was still cut straight across my forehead
I played about the front gate, pulling flowers.
You came by on bamboo stilts, playing horse,
You walked about my seat, playing with blue plums.
And we went on living in the village of Chokan:
Two small people, without dislike or suspicion.

At fourteen I married My Lord you.
I never laughed, being bashful.
Lowering my head, I looked at the wall.
Called to, a thousand times, I never looked back.

At fifteen I stopped scowling,
I desired my dust to be mingled with yours
Forever and forever and forever.
Why should I climb the look out?

At sixteen you departed,
You went into far Ku-to-yen, by the river of swirling eddies,
And you have been gone five months.
The monkeys make sorrowful noise overhead.

You dragged your feet when you went out.
By the gate now, the moss is grown, the different mosses,
Too deep to clear them away!
The leaves fall early this autumn, in wind.
The paired butterflies are already yellow with August
Over the grass in the West garden;
They hurt me. I grow older.
If you are coming down through the narrows of the river Kiang,
Please let me know beforehand,
And I will come out to meet you
                    As far as Cho-fu-Sa.

By Rihaku

EZRA POUND

Toads

Why should I let the toad *work*
        Squat on my life?
Can't I use my wit as a pitchfork
        And drive the brute off?

Six days of the week it soils
        With its sickening poison—
Just for paying a few bills!
        That's out of proportion.

Lots of folk live on their wits:
        Lecturers, lispers,
Losels, loblolly-men, louts—
        They don't end as paupers;

Lots of folk live up lanes
        With fires in a bucket,
Eat windfalls and tinned sardines—
        They seem to like it.

Their nippers have got bare feet,
        Their unspeakable wives
Are skinny as whippets—and yet
        No one actually *starves*.

Ah, were I courageous enough
        To shout *Stuff your pension!*
But I know, all too well, that's the stuff
        That dreams are made on:

For something sufficiently toad-like
        Squats in me, too;
Its hunkers are heavy as hard luck,
        And cold as snow,

And will never allow me to blarney
    My way to getting
The fame and the girl and the money
    All at one sitting.

I don't say, one bodies the other
    One's spiritual truth;
But I do say it's hard to lose either,
    When you have both.

PHILIP LARKIN

Parlour-Piece

With love so like fire they dared not
Let it out into strawy small talk;
With love so like a flood they dared not
Let out a trickle lest the whole crack,

These two sat speechlessly:
Pale cool tea in tea-cups chaperoned
Stillness, silence, the eyes
Where fire and flood strained.

TED HUGHES

Spell of Creation

Within the flower there lies a seed,
Within the seed there springs a tree,
Within the tree there spreads a wood.

In the wood there burns a fire,
And in the fire there melts a stone,
Within the stone a ring of iron.

Within the ring there lies an O
Within the O there looks an eye,
In the eye there swims a sea,

And in the sea reflected sky,
And in the sky there shines the sun,
Within the sun a bird of gold.

Within the bird there beats a heart,
And from the heart there flows a song,
And in the song there sings a word.

In the word there speaks a world,
A word of joy, a world of grief,
From joy and grief there springs my love.

O love, my love, there springs a world,
And on the world there shines a sun
And in the sun there burns a fire,

Within the fire consumes my heart
And in my heart there beats a bird,
And in the bird there wakes an eye,

Within the eye, earth, sea and sky,
Earth, sky and sea within an O
Lie like the seed within the flower.

KATHLEEN RAINE

Alfred Corning Clark

(1916–1961)

You read the *New York Times*
Every day at recess,
but in its dry
obituary, a list
of your wives, nothing is news,
except the ninety-five
thousand dollar engagement ring
you gave the sixth.
Poor rich boy,
you were unseasonably adult
at taking your time,
and died at forty-five.
Poor Al Clark,
Behind your enlarged,
hardly recognisable photograph,
I feel the pain.
You were alive. You are dead.
You wore bow-ties and dark
blue coats, and sucked
wintergreen or cinnamon lifesavers
to sweeten your breath.
There must be something—
some one to praise
your triumphant diffidence,
your refusal of exertion,
the intelligence
that pulsed in the sensitive,
pale concavities of your forehead.
You never worked,
and were third in the form.
I owe you something—
I was befogged,
and you were too bored,

quick and cool to laugh.
You are dear to me, Alfred;
our reluctant souls united
in our unconventional
illegal games of chess
on the St Mark's quadrangle.
You usually won—
motionless
as a lizard in the sun.

ROBERT LOWELL

The Fury of Aerial Bombardment

You would think the fury of aerial bombardment
Would rouse God to relent; the infinite spaces
Are still silent. He looks on shock-pried faces.
History, even, does not know what is meant.

You would feel that after so many centuries
God would give man to repent; yet he can kill
As Cain could, but with multitudinous will,
No further advanced than in his ancient furies.

Was man made stupid to see his own stupidity?
Is God by definition indifferent, beyond us all?
Is the eternal truth man's fighting soul
Wherein the Beast ravens in its own avidity?

Of Van Wettering I speak, and Averill,
Names on a list, whose faces I do not recall
But they are gone to early death, who late in school
Distinguished the belt feed lever from the belt holding pawl.

RICHARD EBERHART

CONNECTIONS

I suggest some possible groupings of poems, and I have further indicated some possible pairings and comparisons within each group. In many groups the emphasis is on the manifest subject of the poem—as in People, Places, Creatures. Regard the subject as a way into the poem. Ask yourself: what is the poet doing with the subject? Is he making a picture? recapturing an experience and teasing out what it meant to him? creating an equivalent to a mood or state of mind? expressing a feeling or conviction? persuading us to share it? Does the subject give him a springboard for a train of thought, or a switchback ride of free association? How—in his rhythms, his choice of words, his tone of voice, his images—does he realize his picture, his mood, his train of thought, his switchback ride?

There is nothing authoritative, nothing hard and fast about these groups. The exploration of a poem may start anywhere; the one place it should not end in is a prose paraphrase. It should end in a discovery of what this poem is, in itself; and it may then go on to a new beginning, a poem which you may write, which will not be just a copy or echo of the poems in this book, but a new thing, in the making of which the older poets will have helped you by showing what words, rhythms and images can do.

There are a few poems that I have not allotted to any group. I could fit Yeats's *Coole Park and Ballylee* (page 148) into Creation, or Places, or Time Passing; but I prefer to leave it alone in the body of the book as a sign that poems are not objects to be slotted into categories, rounded up in groups, slung around the classroom or lobbed back at the examiner. They are independent creations, and they exist to be experienced and to increase our sense of life.

PEOPLE

Old women, tramps, a rich New Yorker, a Chinese wife, two Welsh countrymen, a van-driver, a boozer, a poet, a New Englander, a withdrawn girl, two Real Ladies—how has the poet painted his portraits: by what use of words and rhythms, what choice of detail?

Notice how both these speakers reveal themselves through their words—she is a *lady* not a woman; Job Davies is earthy, but not earth-bound:

R. S. Thomas: Lore	*page*	66
John Betjeman: In Westminster Abbey		70

Here the speaker, as he talks about other people, is giving himself away:

George Mackay Brown: Ikey on the People of Hellya	111
James Stephens: A Glass of Beer	129

A person who describes herself through her concern for another:

Ezra Pound: The River Merchant's Wife: A Letter	158

A sharp self-scrutiny:

Robert Graves: The Face in the Mirror	37

Contrasting views of the old:

Iain Crichton-Smith: Old Woman	22
William Empson: To an Old Lady	110

A machine, and the gear that goes with it, puts its stamp on a man, and on his idea of what he is, or would like to be.

R. S. Thomas: Cynddylan on a Tractor	18
Thom Gunn: Black Jackets	60

Two ways of looking at a man: by his school contemporary, and by a newspaper obituary:

Robert Lowell: Alfred Corning Clark	162

A man and two women, well-bred and sensitive, who can't make any significant contact with other people—and Prufrock knows it:

      T. S. Eliot: The Love Song of J. Alfred Prufrock page 72
      Ezra Pound: The Garden 77
      Sylvia Plath: Spinster 98

RELATIONS

I use the word both in the sense of one's relations, one's family; and in the sense of one's relations *with* one's family and others who are close, such as friends or lovers.

First, parents and children. The first three poems are from the parent's point of view:

      Louis Simpson: The Goodnight 38
      C. Day Lewis: Walking Away 61
      Thom Gunn: Jesus and His Mother 90

And these from the child's:

      R. S. Thomas: Mother and Son 25
      Seamus Heaney: Digging 31
      Sylvia Plath: The Disquieting Muses 85
      Louis Simpson: My Father in the Night Commanding
      No 88

Two husbands and wives:

      Ted Hughes: Her Husband 36
      Ezra Pound: The River Merchant's Wife: A Letter 158

Grandparents: one poem from the grandfather's point of view, one from the grandson's:

      John Crowe Ransom: Old Man Playing with Children 13
      Robert Lowell: Grandparents 140

A family at time of stress:

      Seamus Heaney: Mid-Term Break 51
      D. J. Enright: First Death 62
      John Crowe Ransom: Dead Boy 130

Three pairs of lovers:
Seamus Heaney: *Twice Shy*   *page* 40
Robert Frost: *Two Look at Two*   79
Ted Hughes: *Parlour-Piece*   160

COMMUNITIES

Poems which give a picture of a community—the Orkney
farmers and fishers of George Mackay Brown's poems—or
group of like-minded persons, like the horse-loving gentry
of Keith Douglas's "Aristocrats".

George Mackay Brown: *The Funeral of Ally Flett*   27
D. J. Enright: *Brush-Fire*   56
Louis MacNeice: *Bagpipe Music*   64
George Mackay Brown: *Ikey on the People of Hellya*   111
Louis MacNeice: *Birmingham*   118
Keith Douglas: *Aristocrats*   132
Edwin Muir: *Suburban Dream*   151

Poems which are concerned with a person's relationship to
his community, school, neighbours, country, fellow-men.
"Who *is* my neighbour?" is a question asked, in different
ways, by Auden's "A Summer Night" and Betjeman's
"In Westminster Abbey":

Richard Kell: *The Pay is Good*   11
R. S. Thomas: *Tramp*   15
Louis Simpson: *The Heroes*   46
W. B. Yeats: *Easter 1916*   48
John Betjeman: *In Westminster Abbey*   70
Charles Causley: *Ballad of the Bread Man*   82
W. H. Auden: *A Summer Night*   105

PLACES

The place is the starting point; where does each poem go on
from there?

John Betjeman: *Parliament Hill Fields*   113
Louis MacNeice: *Birmingham*   118

Norman MacCaig: *Edinburgh Courtyard in July*   page   44
Richard Wilbur: *Piazza di Spagna, Early Morning*   45
T. S. Eliot: *Preludes*   136

Vernon Watkins: *Waterfalls*   20
T. S. Eliot: *Rannoch by Glencoe*   41
Dylan Thomas: *Fern Hill*   96
Herbert Read: *The Ivy and the Ash*   128
Andrew Young: *Black Rock of Kiltearn*   140
Iain Crichton-Smith: *By Ferry to the Island*   152

CREATURES

Relationships are involved in some of these poems too: between man and the creatures of:

Seamus Heaney: *The Early Purges*   54
C. Day Lewis: *Circus Lion*   81
Philip Larkin: *Take One Home for the Kiddies*   101
Edward Thomas: *The Gallows*   138

What attitudes to the deaths of creatures do the poems by Larkin, Heaney and Thomas show? And also these two:

Ted Walker: *Easter Poem*   47
George Mackay Brown: *Hawk*   102

Likeness, and unlikeness, between man and the animals:

David Holbrook: *Me and the Animals*   52
Thom Gunn: *On the Move*   124
Michael Roberts: *Images of Death*   127

MAN AND NATURE

Some forces of nature: independent of man—

Roy Campbell: *Horses on the Camargue*   58
Norman MacCaig: *Spate in Winter Midnight*   135
Andrew Young: *Black Rock of Kiltearn*   140

—or working through man:

Wilfred Owen: Futility   page 87
D. H. Lawrence: Song of a Man who has Come Through   95
Louis MacNeice: Spring Voices   134
Gregory Corso: Man About to Enter Sea   150
Kathleen Raine: Spell of Creation   161

Man's attitude to nature: mastering, exploiting or living in harmony:

R. S. Thomas: Cynddyllan on a Tractor   18
Vachel Lindsay: The Flower-fed Buffaloes   125
Marianne Moore: The Arctic Ox (or Goat)   145

W. H. Auden: On This Island   78
Robert Frost: Two Look at Two   79
Dylan Thomas: Fern Hill   96
W. H. Auden: A Summer Night   105

Nature reflecting human moods:

Peter Redgrove: For No Good Reason   53
Charles Madge: Fortune   131

Mysterious forces, that come from beyond the natural world. How are we made to feel these forces?

R. S. Thomas: Genealogy   55
Kathleen Raine: Northumbrian Sequence: IV   68
Sylvia Plath: The Bull of Bendylaw   123
Edwin Muir: Horses   143
Ted Hughes: A Dream of Horses   154

MYTH AND LEGEND

Some poems which contain references to myths and legends. What is their part in the poem, and how do they affect you as you read it?

W. B. Yeats: Lullaby   29
Louis MacNeice: Perseus   33

Louis Simpson: The Goodnight   page 38
D. H. Lawrence: Bavarian Gentians   94
Norman MacCaig: Spate in Winter Midnight   135

Poems which recall a legend or a fairy-tale, or create a new
one. Several are in ballad form. (Here is the place to say
how sorry I was not to be able to include one of the best of
modern ballads, Vernon Watkins's *Ballad of the Mari Lwyd*;
but it would have taken up 25 pages and there was not room
in this short anthology. It is published by Faber in a book of
the same title, and also included in *The Penguin Book of
Longer Modern Verse*.) What happens inside a person—an
overwhelming feeling, a tension, a conflict—is turned into a
drama or tale outside. Does this drama or tale define some-
thing that could not be defined otherwise?

Charles Causley: A Ballad for Katharine of Aragon   23
Edwin Muir: The Bridge of Dread   34
Sylvia Plath: The Disquieting Muses   85
Edwin Muir: Merlin   100
W. H. Auden: O Where are You Going?   101
Sylvia Plath: The Bull of Bendylaw   123
Michael Roberts: The Caves   142

Or an old tale is given a new twist, to bring out a fresh truth:

Charles Causley: Ballad of the Bread Man   82
W. H. Auden: The Shield of Achilles   115
John Short: Carol   138
Roy Fuller: The Hero   157

CREATION

The making and nature of art and poetry; the creation of
order and beauty:

Hugh MacDiarmid: Better One Golden Lyric   30
Edward Thomas: The Unknown   114
W. B. Yeats: Sailing to Byzantium   121
          The Choice   128

Relations between art and life:

W. H. Auden: *Musée des Beaux Arts*　　　　*page* 16
D. J. Enright: *A Polished Performance*　　　　35
Keith Douglas: *Encounter with a God*　　　　104
Richard Eberhart: *Hoot Owls*　　　　109
W. H. Auden: *The Shield of Achilles*　　　　115
T. S. Eliot: *La Figlia che Piange*　　　　120

WORK

Work may mean creation, or just trudging through a dreary job to the goal of a pension. It may involve a person entirely, or be only a minor concern. It may add to a life, or narrow it. It produces strong feelings: what's the point? is it any use?

Richard Kell: *The Pay is Good*　　　　11
Ted Hughes: *Her Husband*　　　　36
R. S. Thomas: *Lore*　　　　66
Philip Larkin: *Toads*　　　　159

W. B. Yeats: *The Scholars*　　　　26
　　　　　　What Then?　　　　42
Ezra Pound: *Salutation*　　　　99
　　　　　　The Lake Isle　　　　99

Are thinking and writing "work" like digging and selling?

Seamus Heaney: *Digging*　　　　31
Edwin Muir: *Suburban Dream*　　　　151

Fantasies of life without work:

Louis MacNeice: *Bagpipe Music*　　　　64

LOVE

As a feeling:

W. B. Yeats: *Lullaby*　　　　29
Robert Graves: *Lost Love*　　　　43
Michael Roberts: *Question and Answer*　　　　45
Ted Hughes: *The Dove-Breeder*　　　　80

John Manifold: Fife Tune   page 103
  Robert Graves: Spoils   156

As a relationship:
  Seamus Heaney: Twice Shy   40
  Ezra Pound: The River Merchant's Wife: A Letter   158
  Ted Hughes: Parlour-Piece   160

And why a "Love Song"?
  T. S. Eliot: The Love Song of J. Alfred Prufrock   72

DEATH

Birth and death are two experiences which come to us all. The
first close encounter with death alters us; our world is dis-
rupted. How do we really experience the death of others? And
how are we encouraged to experience it? Are there conventional
ways of reacting to it—treating death in battle as glorious, for
instance—that may not represent our true feelings?

Death at home:
  Seamus Heaney: Mid-Term Break   51
  D. J. Enright: First Death   62
  John Crowe Ransom: Dead Boy   130

The ceremonies of death:
  William Plomer: Miss Robinson's Funeral   12
  D. H. Lawrence: Giorno dei Morti   19
  George Mackay Brown: The Funeral of Ally Flett   27

Death in War:
  Charles Causley: A Ballad for Katharine of Aragon   23
  W. B. Yeats: Easter 1916   48
  Wilfred Owen: Strange Meeting   63
                  Futility   87
                  The Next War   108
  Stephen Spender: Ultima Ratio Regum   126
  Keith Douglas: Aristocrats   132
                  Vergissmeinicht   144
  Richard Eberhart: The Fury of Aerial Bombardment   163

In its rhythm this echoes the Scottish lament, *The Flowers of the Forest*: and a memory of that poem can affect one's response to this:

    Louis Simpson: The Heroes   *page* 46

TIME AND CHANGE

The passing of time as measured in centuries and generations:

T. S. Eliot: Rannoch, by Glencoe	41
R. S. Thomas: Genealogy	55
Edwin Muir: Merlin	100
Vachel Lindsay: The Flower-fed Buffaloes	125
Michael Roberts: The Caves	142

Time passing in the life of individuals: what feelings does it arouse?

Vernon Watkins: Waterfalls	20
Philip Larkin: Next, Please	21
Iain Crichton-Smith: Old Woman	22
Robert Graves: The Face in the Mirror	37
W. B. Yeats: What Then?	42
C. Day Lewis: Walking Away	61
Dylan Thomas: Fern Hill	96

THINKING IN POETRY

How are ideas embodied and handled in these poems? Is anything being done in verse that couldn't equally well be done in a piece of reasoned prose?

Philip Larkin: Next, Please	21
Hugh MacDiarmid: The Bonnie Broukit Bairn	82
Philip Larkin: Places, Loved Ones	92
William Empson: To an Old Lady	110
Thom Gunn: On the Move	124
Louis MacNeice: Snow	133
Marianne Moore: The Arctic Ox (or Goat)	145
Gregory Corso: Man About to Enter Sea	150
Richard Eberhart: The Fury of Aerial Bombardment	163

AUTHOR INDEX

W. H. AUDEN b. 1907

Musée des Beaux Arts	page 16
On This Island	78
O Where are You Going?	101
A Summer Night	105
The Shield of Achilles	115

Collected Shorter Poems 1927–1957
Faber, 1966

The Shield of Achilles: In Book 18 of Homer's Iliad, the goddess Thetis asks Hephaestos, the lame armourer of the Gods, to make armour for her son Achilles: the shield there described showed beautiful cities, rich fields and vineyards, weddings and dances—and also battle, ambush, strife and panic.

JOHN BETJEMAN b. 1906

In Westminster Abbey	70
Parliament Hill Fields	113

Collected Poems, Murray, 1958

ELIZABETH BISHOP b. 1911

The Map	67

Selected Poems, Chatto & Windus, 1967

GEORGE MACKAY BROWN b. 1921

The Funeral of Ally Flett   *page* 27
The Hawk   102
Ikey on the People of Hellya   111

The Year of the Whale, Hogarth Press, 1965

George Mackay Brown belongs to, and writes about, the
Orkney Islands.

ROY CAMPBELL 1902–1957

Horses on the Camargue   58

Sons of the Mistral, Faber 1941
(*by permission of Curtis Brown Ltd.*)

"*Camargue.* Pampa at the mouth of the Rhône which
together with the Sauvage and the desert Crau forms a
vast grazing ground for thousands of wild cattle and
horses. The Camarguais horses are a distinct race.
Trident. Dual allusion to the trident of Neptune and that
carried by the guardians or cowboys of the Camargue":
Author's note.

CHARLES CAUSLEY b. 1918

A Ballad for Katharine of Aragon   23

Union Street, Rupert Hart-Davis,
1957

Ballad of the Bread Man   82

Underneath the Water,
Macmillan, 1968 (*by permission* of
*The Macmillan Company of Canada
and Macmillan, London*)

GREGORY CORSO b. 1930

Man About to Enter Sea   *page* 150

Selected Poems,
Eyre and Spottiswoode, 1962

IAIN CRICHTON-SMITH b. 1928

Old Woman   22
By Ferry to the Island   152

Thistles and Roses,
Eyre and Spottiswoode, 1961

C. DAY LEWIS b. 1904

Walking Away   61
Circus Lion   81

The Gate, Cape, 1962

KEITH DOUGLAS 1920–1944

Encounter with a God   104
Aristocrats   132
Vergissmeinicht   144

Collected Poems, Faber, 1967

Keith Douglas fought in a tank regiment during the North African campaign in the 1939–45 war. He wrote *Encounter with a God* when he was sixteen.

The epigraph to *Aristocrats* consists of the supposed last words of the Roman Emperor Vespasian.

Vergissmeinicht is the German for "forget-me-not".

RICHARD EBERHART b. 1904

Hoot Owls   109

The Fury of Aerial Bombardment   *page* 163

Collected Poems,
Chatto & Windus, 1960

T. S. ELIOT 1888–1965

Rannoch, by Glencoe   41
The Love Song of J. Alfred Prufrock   72
La Figlia che Piange   120
Preludes   136
Marina   155

Collected Poems, 1909–1962,
Faber, 1963

Rannoch, by Glencoe recalls the massacre of the Mac-
donalds by Government troops in 1692.

The epigraph to *Prufrock* is from Book XXV II of
Dante's Inferno, where the words are spoken by a soul
tormented in hell, when Dante asks him who he is: "If I
thought my answer were to one who ever could return to
the world, this flame should shake no more: but since, if
what I hear be true, none ever did return alive from this
depth without fear of infamy I answer thee."

La Figlia che Piange means "the weeping girl", and the
epigraph is from Vergil's Aeneid, Book 1, where Aeneas
addresses Venus: "Maiden, by what name shall I know
you?"

Marina refers to the reunion of King Pericles with his
daughter Marina, long thought lost at sea, in Shake-
speare's *Pericles*. The epigraph comes from a play by
Seneca: "What is this place, what country, what quarter
of the world?"

WILLIAM EMPSON b. 1906

To an Old Lady   110

Collected Poems,
Chatto & Windus, 1955

D. J. ENRIGHT b. 1920

    A Polished Performance   *page* 35

        Some Men are Brothers,
        Chatto & Windus, 1960

    Brush-Fire   56

        Addictions, Chatto & Windus,
        1962

    First Death   62

        The Laughing Hyena,
        Routledge & Kegan Paul, 1953

D. J. Enright has spent many years teaching in the Far
East: Japan, Thailand, Singapore.

ROBERT FROST 1875–1963

    Two Look at Two   79

        *The Complete Poems of Robert
        Frost*, Cape, 1951

ROY FULLER b. 1914

    The Hero   157

        Collected Poems, 1936–1961
        Deutsch, 1962

ROBERT GRAVES b. 1895

    The Face in the Mirror   37
    Lost Love   43
    Spoils   156

        Collected Poems 1965, Cassell,
        1965 (*by permission of Mr Robert
        Graves*)

THOM GUNN b. 1929

Black Jackets   *page* 60
"Blackie, the Electric Rembrandt"   153
            My Sad Captains, Faber, 1961

Jesus and His Mother   90
On the Move   124
        The Sense of Movement, Faber, 1957

SEAMUS HEANEY b. 1939

Digging   31
Twice Shy   40
Mid-Term Break   51
The Early Purges   54
        Death of a Naturalist, Faber, 1967

DAVID HOLBROOK b. 1923

Me and the Animals   52

            Imaginings, Putnam, 1960
            *(by permission of Mr David
                            Holbrook)*

TED HUGHES b. 1930

Of Cats   14
A Dream of Horses   154
                Lupercal, Faber, 1960

Her Husband   36
                Wodwo, Faber, 1967

The Dove-Breeder   80
Parlour-Piece   160
        The Hawk in the Rain, Faber, 1957

RICHARD KELL b. 1927

    The Pay is Good   *page* 11
        Control Tower, Hogarth Press, 1962

PHILIP LARKIN b. 1922

    Next, Please   21
    Places, Loved Ones   92
    Toads   159
        The Less Deceived,
        Marvell Press, 1955

    Take One Home for the Kiddies   101
        The Whitsun Weddings, Faber, 1964

D. H. LAWRENCE 1885–1930

    Giorno dei Morti   19
    Bavarian Gentians   94
    Song of a Man Who Has Come Through   95
        The Complete Poems of D. H. Lawrence,
        Heinemann, 1964 (*by permission of Laurence*
        Pollinger Ltd., and the Estate of the late
        Mrs Frieda Lawrence)

Giorno dei Morti is "the day of the dead" or All Souls day, November 2, when in Catholic countries graves are visited and decorated by the relations of the dead.

VACHEL LINDSAY 1978–1932

    The Flower-Fed Buffaloes   125
        Going to the Stars, 1926 (*by permission of*
    Appleton-Century affiliate of Meredith Press.
        Copyright 1926 by D. Appleton & Co.
    Copyright renewed 1954 by Elizabeth C. Lindsay).

ROBERT LOWELL b. 1917

Grandparents   *page* 140

Life Studies, Faber, 1959

Alfred Corning Clark   162

For the Union Dead, Faber, 1965

NORMAN MacCAIG b. 1910

Edinburgh Courtyard in July   44
Spate in Winter Midnight   135

A Common Grace, Hogarth Press,
1960

HUGH MacDIARMID b. 1892

Better One Golden Lyric   30
The Bonnie Broukit Bairn   82

Collected Poems,
Oliver and Boyd, 1962
(*by permission of The Macmillan
Company of New York*)

LOUIS MacNEICE 1907–1963

Perseus   33
Bagpipe Music   64
Birmingham   118
Snow   133
Spring Voices   134

Collected Poems, Faber, 1966

CHARLES MADGE b. 1912

Fortune   131

The Disappearing Castle, Faber, 1937

181

JOHN MANIFOLD b. 1915

    Fife Tune   *page* 103

Selected Verse, The John Day
Company Inc., 1946

MARIANNE MOORE b. 1887

    I May, I Might, I Must   56
    The Arctic Ox (or Goat)   145

Complete Poems, Faber, 1968

EDWIN MUIR 1887–1959

    The Bridge of Dread   34
    Merlin   100
    Horses   143
    Suburban Dream   151

Collected Poems, Faber, 1960

WILFRED OWEN 1893–1918

    Strange Meeting   63
    Futility   87
    The Next War   108

Collected Poems, Chatto & Windus,
1963 (*by permission of Mr Harold
Owen*)

Wilfred Owen served for two years on the Western
Front in the War of 1914–1918.

SYLVIA PLATH 1932–1963

    The Disquieting Muses   85
    Spinster   98
    The Bull of Bendylaw   123

The Colossus, Faber, 1967
(*by permission of Olwyn Hughes*)

WILLIAM PLOMER b. 1903

    Miss Robinson's Funeral   *page* 12

            Collected Poems, Cape, 1960

EZRA POUND b. 1885

    The Garden   77
    Salutation   99
    The Lake Isle   99
    The River Merchant's Wife: A Letter   158

            Collected Shorter Poems, Faber, 1968

The River Merchant's Wife is a free version of a poem by a Chinese poet of the eighth century.

KATHLEEN RAINE b. 1908

    Northumbrian Sequence: IV   68
    Spell of Creation   161

            Collected Poems, Hamish Hamilton,
                        1956

JOHN CROWE RANSOM b. 1888

    Old Man Playing with Children   13
    Dead Boy   130

            Selected Poems, Eyre & Spottiswoode,
                        1947

HERBERT READ b. 1893

    The Ivy and the Ash   128

            Collected Poems, Faber, 1966

PETER REDGROVE b. 1932

    For No Good Reason   *page* 53
            The Nature of Cold Weather,
            Routledge & Kegan Paul, 1961

MICHAEL ROBERTS 1902–1948

    Question and Answer   45
    The Images of Death   127
    The Caves   142
            Collected Poems, Faber, 1958

JOHN SHORT b. 1911

    Carol   138
            The Oak and the Ash, Dent, 1947
             (by permission of John Short)

LOUIS SIMPSON b. 1923

    The Goodnight   38
    The Heroes   46
    My Father in the Night Commanding No   88
                    Selected Poems,
          Oxford University Press, 1966

STEPHEN SPENDER b. 1909

    The Express   17
    Ultima Ratio Regum   126
          Collected Poems 1928–1953,
                   Faber, 1955

Ultima Ratio Regum, "the final argument of kings", were the words inscribed on the cannons of the Kings of France.

JAMES STEPHENS 1883–1950

    A Glass of Beer   *page* 129

Collected Poems, Macmillan, 1954
(by permission of Mrs Iris Wise)

DYLAN THOMAS 1914–1953

    Fern Hill   96

Collected Poems, Dent, 1952
*(by permission of the Trustees for the
copyrights of the late Dylan Thomas)*

EDWARD THOMAS 1878–1917

    No One Cares Less than I   93
    The Unknown   114
    The Gallows   138

Collected Poems, Faber, 1936
(by permission of Miss Myfanwy Thomas)

R. S. THOMAS b. 1913

    Tramp   15

The Bread of Truth,
Rupert Hart-Davis, 1963

    Cynddylan on a Tractor   18

Song at the Year's Turning,
Rupert Hart-Davis, 1955

    Mother and Son   25
    Genealogy   55
    Lore   66

Tares, Rupert Hart-Davis, 1961

TED WALKER b. 1934

Easter Poem *page* 47

Fox on a Barn Door, Cape, 1965

VERNON WATKINS 1906–1967

Waterfalls 20

Affinities, Faber, 1962

RICHARD WILBUR b. 1921

Piazza di Spagna, Early Morning 45

Poems 1943–1956, Faber, 1957

The *Piazza di Spagna* is a square in Rome.

WILLIAM CARLOS WILLIAMS 1883–1963

The Dance 57

Collected Later Poems,
MacGibbon & Kee, 1965

W. B. YEATS 1865–1939

The Scholars 26
Lullaby 29
What Then? 42
Easter 1916 48
Sailing to Byzantium 121
The Choice 128
Coole Park and Ballylee, 1931 148

Collected Poems of W. B. Yeats,
Macmillan, 1952 (*by permission
of Mr M. B. Yeats*)

Easter 1916 commemorates the Rising of Irish patriots
in Dublin.

Coole Park and Ballylee is about two homes: the

house at Coole, on the family estate in Galway, of Lady
Gregory, writer and friend of writers; and the Norman
tower at Ballylee, near by, where Yeats himself lived.

ANDREW YOUNG b. 1885

Black Rock of Kiltearn   *page* 140

Collected Poems, Rupert Hart-Davis,
1960

PUBLISHER'S
ACKNOWLEDGEMENTS

Our thanks are expressed to the authors, publishers and others acknowledged in the Author Index, for permission to use the poems.

The following acknowledgements are also made for certain Canadian market rights: to Random House Inc. for "The Shield of Achilles" by W. H. Auden, from *Collected Shorter Poems 1927–1957*, copyright 1952 by W. H. Auden; to Farrar, Straus & Giroux, Inc. for "The Map" by Elizabeth Bishop from *Collected Poems*, copyright 1940, 1946, 1947, 1948, 1949, 1951, 1952, 1955 by Elizabeth Bishop, and for "Grandparents" by Robert Lowell from *Life Studies*, copyright © 1959 by Robert Lowell and "Alfred Corning Clark" by Robert Lowell from *For the Union Dead*, copyright © 1961 by Robert Lowell; to New Directions Publishing Corporation, New York for "Man About to Enter Sea" by Gregory Corso from *Long Live Man*, © 1961 by New Directions, and for "The Garden", "Salutation", "The Lake Isle" and "The River-Merchant's Wife: A Letter" by Ezra Pound from *Personae*, copyright 1928, 1954 by Ezra Pound; to Holt, Rinehart & Winston, Inc. for "Two Look at Two" by Robert Frost from *Complete Poems of Robert Frost*, copyright 1923 by Holt, Rinehart & Winston, Inc., copyright 1951 by Robert Frost; to Harper & Row, Publishers for "The Dove-Breeder" and "Parlour-Piece" from *The Hawk in the Rain* by Ted Hughes, copyright © 1957 by Ted Hughes; to the Macmillan Company of Canada Ltd. for "A Glass of Beer" by James Stephens from *Collected Poems of James Stephens*; to Harcourt, Brace & World, Inc. for "Piazza di Spagna, Early Morning" by Richard Wilbur from *Things of this World*, © 1956 by Richard Wilbur.

TITLE INDEX

The first page reference is to the text of the poem,
the rest to any mentions of it in Connections or
in the notes in the Author Index.

Alfred Corning Clark   *page* 162, 165
Arctic Ox (or Goat), The   145, 169, 173
Aristocrats   132, 167, 172, 176

Bagpipe Music   64, 167, 171
Ballad for Katharine of Aragon, A   23, 170, 172
Ballad of the Bread Man   82, 167, 170
Bavarian Gentians   94, 170
Better One Golden Lyric   30, 170
Birmingham   118, 167
Black Jackets   60, 165
Black Rock of Kiltearn   140, 168
"Blackie, the Electric Rembrandt"   153
Bonnie Broukit Bairn, The   82, 173
Bridge of Dread, The   34, 170
Brush-Fire   56, 167
Bull of Bendylaw, The   123, 169, 170
By Ferry to the Island   152, 168

Carol   138, 170
Caves, The   142, 170, 173
Choice, The   128, 170
Circus Lion   81, 168
Coole Park and Ballylee, 1931   148, 186
Cynddylan on a Tractor   18, 165, 169

Dance, The   57
Dead Boy   130, 166, 172
Digging   31, 166, 171

189

Disquieting Muses, The   *page* 85, 166, 170
Dove-Breeder, The   80, 172
Dream of Horses, A   154, 169

Early Purges, The   54, 168
Easter 1916   48, 167, 172, 186
Easter Poem   47, 168
Edinburgh Courtyard in July   44, 168
Encounter with a God   104, 171, 176
Express, The   17

Face in the Mirror, The   37, 165, 173
Fern Hill   96, 168, 169, 173
Fife Tune   103, 172
First Death   62, 166, 172
Flower-fed Buffaloes, The   125, 169, 173
For no Good Reason   53, 169
Fortune   131, 169
Funeral of Ally Flett, The   27, 167, 172
Fury of Aerial Bombardment, The   163, 172, 173
Futility   87, 169, 172

Gallows, The   138, 168
Garden, The   77, 166
Genealogy   55, 169, 173
Giorno dei Morti   19, 172, 180
Glass of Beer, A   129, 165
Goodnight, The   38, 166, 170
Grandparents   140, 166

Hawk, The   102, 168
Her Husband   36, 166, 171
Hero, The   157, 170
Heroes, The   46, 167, 173
Hoot Owls   109, 171
Horses   143, 169
Horses on the Camargue   58, 168, 175

I May, I Might, I Must   56
Ikey on the People of Hellya   111, 165, 167

190

Images of Death, The   *page* 127, 168
In Westminster Abbey   70, 165, 167
Ivy and the Ash, The   128, 168

Jesus and His Mother   90, 166

La Figlia che Piange   120, 171, 177
Lake Isle, The   99, 171
Lore   66, 165, 171
Lost Love   43, 171
Love Song of J. Alfred Prufrock, The   72, 166, 172, 177
Lullaby   29, 169, 171

Man About to Enter Sea   150, 169, 173
Map, The   67
Marina   155, 177
Me and the Animals   52, 168
Merlin   100, 170, 173
Mid-Term Break   51, 166, 172
Miss Robinson's Funeral   12, 172
Mother and Son   25, 166
Musée des Beaux Arts   16, 171
My Father in the Night Commanding No   88, 166

Next, Please   21, 173
Next War, The   108, 172
No one cares less than I   93
Northumbrian Sequence: IV   68, 169

O Where are You Going?   101, 170
Of Cats   14
Old Man Playing with Children   13, 166
Old Woman   22, 165, 173
On the Move   124, 168, 173
On This Island   78, 169

Parliament Hill Fields   113, 167
Parlour-Piece   160, 167, 172
Pay is Good, The   11, 167, 171
Perseus   33, 169

191

Piazza di Spagna, Early Morning   *page* 45, 168, 186
Places, Loved Ones   92, 173
Polished Performance, A   35, 171
Preludes   136, 168

Question and Answer   45, 171

Rannoch, by Glencoe   41, 168, 173, 177
River Merchant's Wife, The: A Letter   158, 165, 166
                                               172, 183

Sailing to Byzantium   121, 170
Salutation   99, 171
Scholars, The   26, 171
Shield of Achilles, The   115, 170, 171, 174
Snow   133, 173
Song of a Man Who has Come Through   95, 169
Spate in Winter Midnight   135, 168, 170
Spell of Creation   161, 169
Spinster   98, 166
Spoils   156, 172
Spring Voices   134, 169
Strange Meeting   63, 172
Suburban Dream   151, 167, 171
Summer Night, A   105, 167, 169

Take One Home for the Kiddies   101, 168
To an Old Lady   110, 165, 173
Toads   159, 171
Tramp   15, 167
Twice Shy   40, 167, 172
Two Look at Two   79, 167, 169

Ultima Ratio Regum   126, 172, 184
Unknown, The   114, 170

Vergissmeinicht   144, 172, 176

Walking Away   61, 166, 173
Waterfalls   20, 168, 173
What Then?   42, 171, 173